RENAL DIET and LOW-SODIUM SLOW COOKER

The Ultimate Cookbook & 21-Day Meal Plan for Kidney Disease & Diabetes - Delicious Low-Salt & Low-Potassium Recipes for a Healthy Heart – Vegan Dishes Included

liable for any hardship or damages that may befall them after undertaking information described herein.

Additionally, the information in the following pages is intended only for informational purposes and should thus be thought of as universal. As befitting its nature, it is presented without assurance regarding its prolonged validity or interim quality. Trademarks that are mentioned are done without written consent and can in no way be considered an endorsement from the trademark holder.

Introduction

Kidneys, the natural filters of the human body, are responsible for purifying the blood and making it free from metabolic waste, excess water, and toxins. If we examine the internal mechanism of our kidneys, we can see there is a very delicate balance maintained inside of them to allow the waste to release outside of the body. This balance is a result from the concentration of sodium, potassium, and a few other trace minerals around the kidney cells, known as nephron.

When people ask me how a renal diet can prevent kidney diseases, the answer to their question is simple: this diet essentially helps maintain the vital balance of the kidneys. It minimizes the consumption of excess minerals, which can otherwise clog the nephrons, and may start depositing inside the kidneys, resulting in kidney stones in the worst-case scenario. That's why we're bringing you yet another book on the renal diet and its effects on your kidneys, after the success of its first version. In this book, a new range of kidney-friendly recipes are shared, which are simple enough to follow and extremely delicious in taste!

Kidney disease though chronic, but it isn't an automatic death sentence, with the right guide, diet, and checkup, one can live a healthy life as though no disease was ever in view.

It is right that before providing a solution to a question, the question itself should be reviewed and understood. So, in the first few chapters of this incredible diet book, the subject kidney disease, its causes, effects, stages would be discussed, which would lead us to renal diet and Direction improve our health with its special procedures.

Diet is a vital part of treatment for CKD, and it can help immensely in slowing the progression of the disease. There are ingredients that help the kidneys function, while others make the kidneys work harder. This book will focus on crowding out the unhealthy with the healthy and helpful. Also, targeting factors like salt and carbohydrate intake is important to reduce the risk of hypertension, diabetes, and other diseases that can result from kidney failure.

This book is designed to help. With over 100 recipes, plus tips and tricks, this book can help us tackle your new challenge together. It describes exactly what you can eat and what you should try to avoid, and features unique meal plans that can be tailored to your needs and likes. It will also provide you with specific diet information, such as the types of fruit with lower potassium, or the dairy choice with lower phosphorus, so you'll understand the best options when you prepare meals and snacks.

In this time of change and uncertainty, the knowledge you gain from these pages will give you the power to take your life into your hands and make changes to benefit you in the short and long term. I hope to educate and inspire you with new, easy ways to change the trajectory of your health. Adopting a kidney-friendly lifestyle can be challenging at first, but following these recipes will reduce the anxiety associated with selecting smart food options for your everyday life. And lest you worry that your new diet is restrictive or unsustainable, I want to assure you that these recipes are both easy and delicious, and they will give you a realistic, satisfying way to make this lifestyle change. This book will guide you each step of the way. In doing so, it will help take the stress of meal planning out of the equation, and help you focus on the truly important things in life

Chapter 1: Diseases that cause kidney problems.

Before stepping further into the depths of the renal diet, let us learn more about our kidneys and how they function. This basic understanding can ensure a better awareness of kidney disease. Our kidneys act just like a filter; in fact, they are the natural filter of the body, which mainly filters the blood running into them with high pressure. There is one kidney on either side of the body; they both work in sync to clean and purify the entire body's blood constantly and consistently. The renal arteries that enter the kidneys also pass by the membranes in it, which only let the harmful excretory products to pass into the ureters of the kidneys and render the blood cleaned and purified. There is another vital function that the kidneys play which is to keep the water and electrolyte balance maintained in the body. If our body has water in excess, the kidneys will release it through urination, and if our body is dehydrated, then more water is retained. This smart mechanism is only possible when a critical mineral balance is maintained inside the kidney cells since the release of water can only occur through osmosis.

Kidney function or renal function are the terms used to explain how well the kidneys function. A healthy individual is born with a pair of kidneys. This is why whenever one of the kidneys lost its functioning it went unnoticed due to the function of the other kidney. But if the kidney functions further drop altogether and reach a level as low as 25 percent, it turns out to be serious for the patients. People who have only one kidney functioning need proper external therapy and in worst cases, a kidney transplant.

Kidney diseases occur when a number of renal cells known as nephrons are either partially or completely damaged and fail to properly filter blood entering in. The gradual damage of the kidney cells can occur due to various reasons, sometimes it is the acidic or toxic build-up inside the kidney over time, at times it is genetic, or the result of other kidney damaging diseases like hypertension (high blood pressure) or diabetes.

CKD or chronic kidney disease is the stage of kidney damage where it fails to filter the blood properly. The term chronic is used to refer to gradual and long-term damage to an organ. Chronic kidney disease is therefore developed after a slow yet progressive damage to the kidneys. The symptoms of this disease only appear when the toxic wastes start to build up in the body. Therefore, such a stage should be prevented at all costs. Hence, early diagnosis of the disease proves to be significant. The sooner the patient realizes the gravity of the situation, the better measures he can take to curb the problem.

There is never a single cause for a disease; a number of factors come into play and together become the source of the renal deficiency. As stated earlier, these causes may include the genetics of a person, some other health disorders that may damage the kidneys and the kind of lifestyle a person lives. The following are the most commonly known causes of renal disease.

Heart disease

Diabetes

Hypertension (High blood pressure)

Being around 60 years old

Having kidney disease in family.

Direction keep your kidneys healthy

Like all other parts of the body, human kidneys also need much care and attention to work effectively. It takes a few simple and consistent measures to keep them healthy. Remember that no medicine can guarantee good health, but only a better lifestyle can do so. Here are a few of the practices that can keep your kidneys stay healthy for life.

Active lifestyle an active routine is imperative for good health. This may include regular exercise, yoga, or sports and physical activities. The more you move your body, the better its metabolism gets. The loss of water is compensated by drinking more water, and that constantly drains all the toxins and waste from the kidneys. It also helps in controlling blood pressure, cholesterol levels, and diabetes, which indirectly prevents kidney disease.

Control blood pressure Constant high blood pressure may cause glomerular damage. It is one of the leading causes, and every 3 out of 5 people suffering from hypertension also suffer from kidney problems. The normal human blood pressure is below 120/80 mmHg. When there is a constant increase of this pressure up to 140/100mmHg or more it should be immediately put under control. This can be done by minimizing the salt intake, controlling the cholesterol level and taking care of cardiac health.

Hydration Drinking more water and salt-free fluids proves to be the life support for kidneys. Water and fluids dilute the blood consistency and lead to more urination; this in turn will release most of the excretions out of the body without much difficulty. Drinking at least eight glasses of water in a day is essential. It is basically the lack of water which strains the kidneys and often hinders the glomerular filtration. Water is the best option, but fresh fruit juices with no salt and preservatives are also vital for kidney health. Keep all of them in constant daily use.

Dietary changes There are certain food items which taken in excess can cause renal problems. In this regard, an extremely high protein diet, food rich in sodium, potassium, and phosphorous can be harmful. People who are suffering from early stages of renal disease should reduce their intake, whereas those facing critical stages of CKD should avoid their use altogether. A well-planned renal diet can prove to be significant in this regard. It effectively restricts all such food items from the diet and promotes the use of more fluids, water, organic fruits, and a low protein meal plan.

No smoking/alcohol Smoking and excessive use of alcohol are other names for intoxication. Intoxication is another major cause of kidney disease, or at least it aggravates the condition. Smoking and drinking alcohol indirectly pollute the blood and body tissues, which leads to progressive kidney damage. Begin by gradually reducing alcohol consumption and smoking down to a minimum.

Monitor the changes Since the early signs of kidney disease are hardly detectable, it is important to keep track of the changes you witness in your body. Even the frequency of urination and loss of appetite are good enough reasons to be cautious and concerning. It is true that only a health expert can accurately diagnose the disease, but personal care and attention to minor changes is of key importance when it comes to CKD.

Direction prevent dialysis naturally

Dialysis steps in as a last case scenario when both kidneys lose sufficient function to clean the blood. Before the toxicity reaches a damaging level, it must be eradicated through external sources. Individuals who suffer from acute kidney diseases end up going through dialysis to get their blood cleaned through the artificial dialysis machine. This dialysis machine mimics the role of our kidneys, and the blood is pumped into the machine, and then it is pumped back into the body simultaneously. People who never went through dialysis should know that it is one long and exhaustive process, which every renal patient hates to go through. Fortunately, there are some effective measures to avoid dialysis. This precautionary measure can stop the progression of renal disease and even cure it to some extent.

Exercise regularly

Don't smoke

Avoid excess salt in your diet

Control of diabetes

Eat correctly and lose excess weight

Control high blood pressure

Talk with your health care team.

Role of potassium, sodium, and phosphorous

Sodium

Sodium is considered the most important electrolyte of the body next to chloride and potassium. The electrolytes are actually the substance that controls the flow of fluids into the cells and out of them. Sodium is mainly responsible for regulating blood volume and pressure. It is also involved in controlling muscle contraction and nerve functions. The acid-base balance in the blood and other body fluids is also regulated by sodium. Though sodium is important for the health and regulation of important body mechanisms, excessive sodium intake, especially when a person suffers from some stages of chronic kidney disease, can be dangerous. Excess sodium disrupts the critical fluid balance in the body and inside the kidneys. It then leads to high blood pressure, which in turn negatively affects the kidneys. Salt is one of the major sources of sodium in our diet, and it is strictly forbidden on the renal diet. High sodium intake can also lead to Edema, which is swelling of the face, hands, and legs. Furthermore, high blood pressure can stress the heart and cause the weakening of its muscles. The build-up of fluid in the lungs also leads to shortness of breath.

Potassium

Potassium is another mineral that is closely linked to renal health. Potassium is another important electrolyte, so it maintains the fluid balance in the body and its pH levels as well. This electrolyte also plays an important role in controlling nerve impulses and muscular activity. It works in conjugation with the sodium to carry out all these functions. The normal potassium level in the blood must range between 3.5 and 5.5mEq/L. It is the kidneys that help maintain this balance, but without their proper function, the potassium starts to build up in the blood. Hyperkalemia is a condition characterized by high potassium levels. It usually occurs in people with chronic kidney disease. The prominent symptoms of high potassium are numbness, slow pulse rate, weakness, and nausea. Potassium is present in green vegetables and some fruits, and these ingredients should be avoided on a renal diet.

Phosphorous

The amount of phosphorus in the blood is largely linked to the functioning of the kidneys. Phosphorus, in combination with vitamin D, calcium, and parathyroid hormone, can regulate the renal function. The balance of phosphorous and calcium is maintained by the kidneys, and this balance keeps the bones and teeth healthy. Phosphorous, along with vitamin D, ensures the absorption of calcium into the bones and teeth, where this mineral is important for the body. On the other hand, it gets dangerous when the kidneys fail to control the amount of phosphorus in the blood. This may lead to heart and bone-related problems. Mainly there is a high risk of weakening of the bones followed by the hardening of the tissues due to the deposition of phosphorous and calcium outside the bones. This abnormal calcification can occur in the lungs, skin, joints, and arteries, which can become in time very painful. It may also result in bone pain and itching.

Chapter 2: The causes

Kidneys are important organs for the human body. They filter out excess water, waste products, and other impurities of the blood. Chronic kidney disease or CKD means your kidneys are damaged and can't filter blood properly. The kidney damage can cause waste to build up in your body. CKD causes many health problems.

Who is at risk of developing CKD?

Diabetes: People with diabetes are prone to CKD. Data shows that about one-third of diabetic patients have CKD.

High blood pressure: About 1 in 5 adults with high blood pressure has CKD.

Heart disease: Recent research shows that there is a link between high blood pressure and kidney disease. People with kidney disease are at a higher risk of heart disease and people with heart disease are at a higher risk of kidney disease.

Family history of kidney failure: People with a family history are at risk for CKD.

Besides this there are other risk factors including

Being Asian-American, Native American, and African-American

Smoking

Old age

Obesity

Stages of renal disease

The five main stages of chronic kidney disease can be categorized as follows:

Stage 1:

The first stage starts when the eGFR gets slightly higher than the normal value. In this stage, the eGFR can be equal or greater than 90mL/min

Stage 2:

The next stage arises when the eGFR starts to decline and ranges between 60 to 89 mL/min. It is best to control the progression of the disease at this point.

Stage 3:

From this point on, the kidney disease becomes concerning for the patient as the eGFR drops to 30-59 mL/min. At this stage, consultation is essential for the health of the patient.

Stage 4:

The stage 4 is also known as Severe Chronic Kidney Diseases as the eGFR level drops to 15-29 mL/min.

Stage 5:

The final and most critical phase of chronic renal disease is stage 5, where the estimated glomerular filtration rate gets as low as below 15 mL/min.

Chapter 3: Diet plan to better experience this problem.

One of the most effective ways to prevent kidney disease is with proper diet.

It's also important to know that those who are at risk of this disease or have already been diagnosed with this condition can help alleviate symptoms and slow down the progression of the disease with a diet called the renal diet.

As you know, the wastes in the blood come from the foods and drinks that you consume.

When your kidneys are not functioning properly, they are unable to remove these wastes efficiently.

Wastes that remain in the blood can negatively affect your overall health.

Following a renal diet can help bolster the functioning of the kidney, reduce damage to the kidneys and prevent kidney failure.

A renal diet is a type of diet that involves consumption of foods and drinks that are low in potassium, sodium and phosphorus.

It also puts focus on the consumption of high-quality protein as well as limiting too much intake of fluids and calcium.

Since each person's body is different, it's important to come up with a specific diet formulated by a dietician to make sure that the diet is tailored to the needs of the patient.

Some of the substances that you have to check and monitor for proper renal diet include:

The Benefits of Renal Diet

A renal diet minimizes intake of sodium, potassium and phosphorus.

Excessive sodium is harmful to people who have been diagnosed with kidney disease as this causes fluid buildup, making it hard for the kidneys to eliminate sodium and fluid.

Improper functioning of the kidneys can also mean difficulty in removing excess potassium.

When there is too much potassium in the body, this can lead to a condition called hyperkalemia, which can also cause problems with the heart and blood vessels.

Kidneys that are not working efficiently find it difficult to remove excess phosphorus.

High levels of phosphorus excrete calcium from the bones causing them to weaken. This also causes elevation of calcium deposits in the eyes, heart, lungs, and blood vessels.

What to Eat and What to Avoid in Renal Diet

A renal diet focuses on foods that are natural and nutritious, but at the same time, are low in sodium, potassium and phosphorus.

Foods to eat:

Cauliflower - 1 cup contains 19 mg sodium, 176 potassium, 40 mg phosphorus

Blueberries - 1 cup contains 1.5 mg sodium, 114 potassium, 18 mg phosphorus

Sea Bass - 3 ounces contain 74 mg sodium, 279 potassium, 211 mg phosphorus

Grapes - 1/2 cup contains 1.5 mg sodium, 144 potassium, 15 mg phosphorus

Egg Whites - 2 egg whites contain 110 mg sodium, 108 potassium, 10 mg phosphorus

Garlic - 3 cloves contain 1.5 mg sodium, 36 potassium, 14 mg phosphorus

Buckwheat - ½ cup contains 3.5 mg sodium, 74 potassium, 59 mg phosphorus

Olive Oil - 1 ounce 0.6 mg sodium, 0.3 potassium, 0 mg phosphorus

Bulgur - ½ cup contains 4.5 mg sodium, 62 potassium, 36 mg phosphorus

Cabbage - 1 cup contains 13 mg sodium, 119 potassium, 18 mg phosphorus

Skinless chicken - 3 ounces contain 63 mg sodium, 216 potassium, 192 mg phosphorus

Bell peppers - 1 piece contains 3 mg sodium, 156 potassium, 19 mg phosphorus

Onion - 1 piece contains 3 mg sodium, 102 potassium, 20 mg phosphorus

Arugula - 1 cup contains 6 mg sodium, 74 potassium, 10 mg phosphorus

Macadamia nuts - 1 ounce contains 1.4 mg sodium, 103 potassium, 53 mg phosphorus

Radish - ½ cup contains 23 mg sodium, 135 potassium, 12 mg phosphorus

Turnips - ½ cup contains 12.5 mg sodium, 138 potassium, 20 mg phosphorus

Pineapple - 1 cup contains 2 mg sodium, 180 potassium, 13 mg phosphorus

Cranberries – 1 cup contains 2 mg sodium, 85 potassium, 13 mg phosphorus

Mushrooms – 1 cup contains 6 mg sodium, 170 potassium, 42 mg phosphorus

Foods to Avoid

These foods are known to have high levels of potassium, sodium or phosphorus:

Soda – Soda is believed to contain up to 100 mg of additive phosphorus per 200 ml.

Avocados - 1 cup contains up to 727 mg of potassium.

Canned foods – Canned foods contain high amounts of sodium so make sure that you avoid using these, or at least, opt for low-sodium versions.

Whole wheat bread – 1 ounce of bread contains 57 mg phosphorus and 69 mg potassium, which is higher compared to white bread.

Brown rice – 1 cup of brown rice contains 154 mg potassium while 1 cup of white rice only has 54 mg potassium.

Bananas – 1 banana contains 422 mg potassium.

Dairy – Dairy products is high in potassium, phosphorus and calcium. You can still consume dairy products but you have to limit it. Use dairy milk alternatives like almond milk and coconut milk.

Processed Meats – Processed meats are not advisable to people with kidney problems because of their high content of additives and preservatives.

Pickled and cured foods – These are made using large amounts of salt.

Apricots – 1 cup contains 427 mg potassium.

Potatoes and sweet potatoes – 1 potato contain 610 mg potassium. You can double boil potatoes and sweet potatoes to reduce potassium by 50 percent.

Tomatoes – 1 cup tomato sauce contains up to 900 mg potassium.

Instant meals – Instant meals are known for extremely high amounts of sodium.

Spinach – Spinach contains up to 290 mg potassium per cup. Cooking helps reduce the amount of potassium.

Raisins, prunes and dates – Dried fruits have concentrated nutrients including potassium. 1 cup prunes contain up to 1,274 mg potassium.

Chips – Chips are known to have high amounts of sodium.

Since the Renal Diet is generally a Low Sodium, Low Phosphorus program, there are certain health benefits that you will enjoy from this diet. (Apart from improving your kidney health). Some of the crucial ones are as follows:

It helps to lower blood pressure

It helps to lower your LDL cholesterol

It helps to lower your risk of having a heart attack

It helps to prevent heart failure

It decreases the possibility of having a stroke

It helps to protect your vision

It helps to improve your memory

It helps to lower the possibility of dementia

It helps to build stronger bones.

Chapter 4: Your Kidneys and Your Health —Understanding Kidney Disease

How is our health dependent on our kidneys? That's what often comes to mind when we overlook the function of our kidneys or take them for granted. Imagine that around the clock, all the waste produced and released into your blood is constantly removed—and not only that, but the kidneys are also responsible for maintaining the fluids and water levels in the body. If you consume a lot of excess water, then the excess is released out of the body by the kidneys, and in case of dehydration, more water is retained inside. All of this can happen if the kidneys are working properly. If not, it can lead to toxic buildup in the body, which can damage kidneys, as well as other organs, and disturb the natural metabolism.

Most people are born with a kidney on each side of the body that work simultaneously to purify the blood, and both support each other in their renal function. Even when one of the kidneys loses 40 percent of its renal function, the other kidney can hide this damage until properly checked and tested. This is the reason patients do not come to know about the renal disease until there is enough damage done. If any of the kidneys loses its renal function below 25 percent, it must raise the alarms, as this is highly dangerous.

Individuals whose renal function decreases to only 15 percent would require an external treatment or dialysis.

Chronic kidney disease is a slow-moving disease and does not cause the patient a lot of complaints in the initial stages. The group of diseases of chronic kidney disease includes several kidney diseases, in which case the renal function decreases for several years or decades. With the help of timely diagnosis and treatment can slow down and even stop the progression of kidney disease.

In international studies of renal function in many people, it was found that almost every tenth kidney was found to have impaired kidney function to one degree or another.

The three most common causes of chronic kidney disease are diabetes, high blood pressure, and glomerulonephritis.

Diabetes - in the case of this disease, various organs are damaged, including the kidneys and heart, as well as blood vessels, nerves, and eyes. With long-term diabetic kidney damage, many patients increase blood pressure and need to be treated accordingly.

High blood pressure (hypertension, primary arterial hypertension) - during hypertension, blood pressure cannot be controlled, and it begins to exceed the limits of the norm (more than 140/90 mm Hg). If this condition is permanent, it can cause chronic kidney disease, brain stroke, or myocardial infarction.

Glomerulonephritis is a disease that occurs as a result of a breakdown in the immune system, during which the filtration function of the kidneys disrupts immune inflammation. The disease can affect only the kidneys and can spread to the entire body (vacuities, lupus nephritis). Glomerulonephritis is often accompanied by high blood pressure.

Many other conditions can cause chronic kidney disease, for example: Hereditary diseases - such as, for example, polycystic kidney disease, due to which over the years a large number of cysts appear in the kidneys, which damage the functioning renal tissue and therefore develop renal failure. Other hereditary diseases of the kidneys are much less common (Alport syndrome, Fabry disease, etc.) problems caused by obstructions in the kidneys and urine excretion - such as congenital malformations of the ureter, kidney stones, tumors or enlargement of the prostate gland in men repeated urinary tract infections or pyelonephritis.

Does everyone have chronic kidney disease?

Chronic kidney disease can develop at any age. The greatest risk of getting sick is in people who have one or more of the following risk factors:

Diabetes

High blood pressure

Family members have previously had kidney disease

Age over 50

Long-term consumption of drugs that can damage the kidneys

Overweight or obesity

What are the symptoms of chronic kidney disease?

If chronic kidney disease progresses, then the blood levels of end products of metabolism increase, this in turn, is the cause of feeling unwell. Various health problems may occur, such as high blood pressure, anemia (anemia), bone disease, premature cardiovascular calcification, discoloration, composition and volume of urine.

As the disease progresses, the main symptoms can be:

Weakness, feeling of weakness

Dyspnea

Trouble sleeping

Lack of appetite

Dry skin, itchy skin

Muscle cramps especially at night

Swelling in the legs

Swelling around the eyes, especially in the morning

Diagnose with Chronic Kidney Disease

To diagnose kidney disease, there are two simple tests that your family doctor can prescribe.

Blood test: glomerular filtration rate (GFR) and serum creatinine level. Creatinine is one of those end products of protein metabolism, the level of which in the blood depends on age, gender, muscle mass, nutrition, physical activity, on which foods before taking the sample (for example, a lot of meat was eaten), and some drugs. Creatinine is excreted from the body through the kidneys, and if the work of the kidneys slows down, the level of creatinine in the blood plasma increases. Determining the level of creatinine alone is not sufficient for the diagnosis of chronic kidney disease since its value begins to exceed the upper limit of the norm only when GFR decreased by half. GFR is calculated using a formula that includes four parameters that take into account the creatinine reading, age, gender, and race of the patient. GFR shows at what level is the ability of the kidneys to filter. In the case of chronic kidney disease, the GFR indicator indicates the stage of the severity of kidney disease.

Urine analysis: the content of albumin in the urine is determined; also, the values of albumin and creatinine in the urine are determined by each other. Albumin is a protein in the urine that usually enters the urine in minimal quantities. Even a small increase in the level of albumin in the urine in some people may be an early sign of incipient kidney disease, especially in those with diabetes and high blood pressure. In the case of normal kidney function, albumin in the urine should be no more than 3 mg/mmol (or 30 mg *g*). *If albumin excretion increases even more, then it already speaks of kidney disease. If albumin excretion exceeds 300 mg* g, other proteins are excreted into the urine, and this condition is called proteinuria.

If the kidney is healthy, then albumin does not enter the urine.

In the case of an injured kidney, albumin begins to enter the urine.

If, after receiving the results of the urine analysis, the doctor suspects that there is a kidney disease, then an additional urine analysis is performed for albumin. If albuminuria or proteinuria is detected again within three months, then this indicates chronic kidney disease.

Additional examinations

In kidney ultrasound examination: in the diagnosis of chronic kidney disease, it is an examination of the primary choice. Ultrasound examination allows to assess the shape of the kidneys, their size, location, as well as to determine possible changes in the kidney tissue and / or other abnormalities that may interfere with the normal functioning of the kidneys. Ultrasound examination of the kidneys does not require special training and has no risks for the patient.

If necessary, and if a urological disease is suspected, an ultrasound examination of the urinary tract can be prescribed (as well as a residual urine analysis), and an ultrasound examination of the prostate gland can be prescribed for men and referred to a urologist for a consultation. If necessary, and if a gynecological disease is suspected, a woman is referred for consultation to a gynecologist.

What you need to know about the examination with a contrast agent, if you have chronic kidney disease Diagnostic examinations such as magnetic resonance imaging, computed tomography, and angiography are used to diagnose and treat various diseases and injuries. In many cases, intravenous and intra-arterial contrast agents (containing iodine or gadolinium) are used, which makes it possible to see the organs or blood vessels under study.

What is particularly important to do before the survey pole to gain in contrast substance?

If you are scheduled for an examination with a contrast agent, then you need to determine your GFR.

Together with your doctor, you can discuss and evaluate the benefits or harm to your health. If the survey is still necessary, follow the following preparation rules:

The day before the survey and the day after the survey, drink plenty of fluids (water, tea, etc.). If you are on treatment in a hospital, then you will be injected with the necessary amount of fluid through a vein by infusion. When staying in hospital treatment after examination with a contrast agent (within 48-96 hours), it is usually prescribed to determine the level of creatinine in the blood to assess renal function. In the outpatient examination with a contrast agent, your family doctor will be able to evaluate your kidney function.

Discuss with your doctor the questions about which medications should not be taken before the examination with a contrast agent. Some drugs (antibiotics, drugs against high blood pressure, etc.) along with contrasting substances begin to act as a poison. The day before and the day after the examination, in no case should you take metformin - a cure for diabetes.

Between the two examinations with a contrast agent, at the first opportunity, sufficient time should be left for the contrast agent that was used during the first examination to leave the body. It is important to exclude repeated examinations with a large amount of contrast material.

Chapter 5: Foods to avoid dialysis

Dialysis is basically a process that helps to get rid of toxin and extra fluid build-up in your body through artificial means. However, an external machine won't really be able to do everything that your kidney can do, so even with dialysis; you might face some complications in the long run.

That being said, there are two types of dialysis.

Peritoneal Dialysis This form of treatment tries to cleanse your blood by utilizing the lining of your abdominal area and cleansing solution known as "Dialysate." The best part about this dialysis is that it can easily be done at home, as long as you have a clean and private area.

Hemodialysis This particular treatment is also known as "Hemo" and is the most common one for kidney failures. This form of dialysis utilizes a machine to filter and clean out your blood. It is recommended that you do this at a hospital; however, if you have the budget, then it is possible to do it at home, as well.

After dialysis is the kidney transplant.

Kidney Transplant A kidney transplant, as the name implies, is essentially surgery that gives you a healthy kidney from a donor's body. It is possible to have a kidney donated from a live body or a donor who has already died but has donated their kidney for a good cause. As mentioned above, if you can get a healthy kidney, then it is possible to lead a completely normal life.

Medical Management If you have budget issues or j want to avoid dialysis or transplant altogether, then there are some medical solutions that you might look into to reduce the symptoms of kidney failure.

They will create a care plan for you that will guide you on what you should do and what you should not do. Make sure to always keep a copy of the plan wherever you go and discuss the terms with your loved ones as well.

It should be noted that most individuals who tend to go for medical management opt for hospice care.

The primary aim of hospice care is to try and decrease your pain and improve the quality of your final days before you die.

In medical management, you can expect a hospice to:

Help you by providing you with a nursing home

Help your family and friends to support you

Try to improve the quality of your life as much as possible

Try to provide medications and care to help you manage your symptoms

But keep in mind that regardless of which path you take, always discuss everything with your doctor.

Learning to Deal with Kidney Failure

Learning that you are suffering from kidney failure might be a difficult thing to cope with. No matter how long you have been preparing for the inevitable, this is something that will come as a shock to you.

But, as mentioned earlier, just because you have started dialysis, doesn't mean that everything that you hold dear has to come to an end!

It might be a little bit difficult at first to get yourself oriented to a new routine, but once you get into the groove, you'll start feeling much better.

Your nurses, loved ones, doctors, and co-workers will all be there to support you.

To make things easier, though, let me break down the individual types of problems that you might face and how you can deal with them.

Stress During Kidney Failure

When you are suffering from kidney failure, it's normal to be stressed out all the time. This might lead you to skip meals or even forgetting your medication, which might affect your health even more.

But you need to understand that life is full of hurdles and setbacks, and you really can't let them hold you back.

In that light, here are six tips to help you keep your stress under control:

Make sure to take some time to just relax and unwind. Try to practice deep breathing, visualization, meditation or even muscle relaxation. All of these will help you to stay calm and keep your body healthy.

Make sure to involve yourself in regular exercise. Take a hike, ride a bicycle or just simply take a jog. They all help. And if those aren't your thing, then you can always go for something more soothing, like tai chi or yoga.

When you are feeling too stressed, try to call up a friend or a beloved family member and talk to them. And if that's not helping, you can always take help from a psychiatrist/counselor.

Try to accept the things that are not under your control, and you can't change. Trying to enforce a change on something that is not within your reach will only make things worse for you. Better advice is to look for better ways of handling the situation instead of trying to change it.

Don't put too much pressure on yourself, try to be good to yourself and don't expect much. You are a human being, after all, right? You can make mistakes, so accept that. Just try your best.

And lastly, always try to maintain a positive attitude. Even when things go completely wrong, try to see the good instead of the bad and focus on that. Try to find things in all phases of your life that make you happy and that you appreciate, such as your friends, work, health and family, for example. You have no idea how much help a simple change of perspective can bring.

Exercise

Apart from the special diet, such as the Renal Diet, physical activity is another way through which you can improve the quality of your life.

This might be a little bit tough to do if you are alone, but it is very much possible. However, you should keep in mind that working out alone won't help you; you must work out and follow a well-balanced, healthy diet.

Both of this combined will go to great lengths to help you lose weight and control your disease.

In fact, a study has shown that people who try to complete 10,1000 steps per day and work out for about 2½ hours every week, while cutting down 500-800 calories per day and following a proper diet routine, have a 50% chance of reducing blood sugar to normal levels, which will further help you to stay healthy.

Common forms of exercise include:

Stair climbing

Tai Chi

Stretching

Yoga

Cycling

Walking

Swimming

To perform these normal workouts, you don't have to join a gym or even buy any sort of expensive equipment! You can simply take a walk around your streets, do yoga at home, and so on.

Just make sure to consult with your doctor to find out which exercise is suitable for you and adjust them to your dialysis routine.

Anxiety and Depression

These two are possibly the most prominent issues that you are going to face. A feeling of depression might last for a long period of time if left unattended. Anxiety might come at the same time, but it won't last for long.

Either way, mood swings will occur that will suddenly make you sad.

However, you should know that it is completely normal to feel anxious or sad when you're going through such a huge change in life. This is even more prominent if you start taking dialysis, as it will require you to completely change your daily routine and follow a different type of diet.

During this adjusting phase, you'll feel many emotions, such as anger, fear, sadness, ETC.

To summarize: The symptoms of depression are:

Loss of interest

Loss of any appetite

Sleeping problems.

On the other hand, symptoms of anxiety are:

Constant sweating

Quick breathing

Inconsistent heartbeat

Constant troubling thoughts

Regardless, the main thing to know is that you are not alone in this fight. Thousands of people have and are going through the same experience. Many people often feel left alone and lose the will to fight, but it doesn't have to be the same for you.

Help is always available! Try sharing with your family members, join support groups, talk to a social worker, ETC.

It doesn't matter what your situation is; if you just reach out to the right person, then you will always find the help and support that you need.

Is it Possible to Work During Dialysis?

Some people often think that you have to stop working or retire from your job the moment you start taking dialysis. But that's not necessarily true.

It is very much possible to keep working even after you start dialysis. In fact, it is recommended that you try to continue working in order to stay happier and healthier.

If your company provides health insurance, then you can even keep enjoying the benefits of insurance while you work. It will help you bear the costs of your dialysis as well.

There are some types of dialysis that provide more flexible treatment options, allowing you to have more time during the day for your job.

Nocturnal (Night-Time) dialysis, either at home or hospital, is perfect for these.

However, if you do start working during your dialysis, you should understand your limits. While you are working, it is possible that you might feel a bit weak or tired.

If you are following peritoneal dialysis, then you are going to need a clean place to do all your exchanges.

Alternatively, if you are on Hemo, then it is strictly prohibited for you to lift heavy objects or put excess pressure on your vascular access arm.

Depending on your dialysis type, you must talk to your social worker/doctor to adjust your dialysis routine and talk to your employer in order to reach an agreement.

Worst case scenario, if you are unable to work, you still have some options! Various federal and private programs will help you to have a stable income while keeping your insurance for your dialysis program.

Talk to your personal social worker in order to apply for these facilities.

The minerals that maintain the internal concentration balance inside the kidneys obviously come from our diet. Salt, the everyday ingredient of our lives, is one of the purest and most direct sources of sodium. There are also other sources of potassium and calcium. By deliberately limiting the intake of such ingredients in our diet, we can manage all our renal problems and even prevent further damage to the kidney cells. Food has a profound impact on your health, and its importance can never be denied. A comprehensive renal diet provides a concrete plan to keep the kidneys healthy and working.

What to Eat and What to Avoid

Some minerals cannot be consumed regularly, or in excess, on the renal diet. Therefore, this diet focuses on specific minerals and their sources, limiting them to a certain extent. There is no restriction on the food, which does not contribute to concentration imbalance in the body. Let's look into the food that can or cannot be consumed on the renal diet in more detail.

Lesser Sodium

Sodium is a major constituent that maintains the internal concentration of the kidney. Its excess can lead to an imbalance that indirectly burdens the kidney and its cells. Sodium is largely present in all the salts that we consume in our diet. For a renal diet, salt is strictly prohibited. But there are several other ingredients as well, which might contain quite a lot of sodium, such as store-bought soup packets, broths, dips, bouillon cubes, and other processed items. It is therefore recommended to at least give their nutritional labels a thorough read before buying them.

Here is the list of ingredients that all contain sodium, and they should certainly be avoided on a renal diet. For some items, like soy sauce or broths, there are low sodium alternatives available in the market which you can use in your diet.

Salt of all types

Processed food

Fast food

Brine-dipped food

Fermented high sodium products

Soy sauce and other high sodium sauces

Herbs and seasonings with sodium

Protein Intake

When metabolized, a protein molecule can release uric acid and other toxins which can, in turn, disrupt the natural balance of the kidneys. The buildup of uric acid, along with other minerals inside the kidneys, can result in kidney stones or renal damage. This is the reason that the renal diet is also restrictive about the consumption of protein. Too much protein intake means a greater buildup of uric acid in the body, which can result in kidney diseases. It is therefore prescribed to limit protein intake to small amounts. Here are a few animals and plant-based sources of proteins: *Animal Protein Foods*

Fish

Chicken

Meat

Eggs

Dairy

When you take them in small amounts per serving, then these proteins will not damage the kidneys. About 2-3 ounces of meat per serving is enough to control the damage, and ½ cup of yogurt, milk, or cheese per serving is enough to keep your kidneys healthy.

Plant Protein Foods

Beans

Nuts

Grains

Similarly, protein from plant sources should be taken in a controlled proportion. Consume only half a cup of beans and half a cup of nuts per serving.

Choose Foods Healthy for Hearts

Renal damage can result in a number of other problems, such as hypertension and high blood pressure. Constant high blood pressure can result in cardiac damage and may cause permanent heart problems. The renal diet also prevents cardiac illnesses and keeps our heart healthy. And to further ensure the good health of the heart, there are certain food items which should be taken regularly on a diet, such as:

Heart-Healthy Foods

Fruits

Beans

Poultry without the skin

Fish

Lean cuts of meat

Vegetables

Low-fat or fat-free milk, yogurt, and cheese

List of Juices and Drinks

Natural and salt-free drinks are best to maintain the internal balance of the kidneys. The more you drink water and other fluids, the more of the toxins and minerals get released out of the kidneys without damaging nephrons. Following are some of the fluids you must drink on a kidney-friendly diet:

Water

Cranberry juice

Apple cider

Grape juice

Lemonade

Fruit Juices You can also try fresh juices from the following fruits:

Apples

Berries

Cherries

Fruit cocktail, drained

Grapes

Peaches

Pears, fresh or canned, drained

Pineapples

Plums

Tangerines

Watermelons

Best Advice to Avoid Dialysis

Dialysis is the artificial process that is used to clean and purify the blood outside of the kidneys. It is a long and excruciating process that most people don't care for. That is why it is suggested to control the renal damage to avoid such extreme conditions. Here are certain tips to avoid dialysis:

Exercise regularly

Eat right and lose excess weight

Don't smoke

Avoid excess salt in your diet

Control high blood pressure

Control diabetes

Talk with your healthcare team

However, in the case of extreme kidney damage, dialysis remains the only option for people.

A Kidney-Friendly Lifestyle

Once a kidney is damaged there is no one-time solution or magic to undo all the damage. It requires constant management and a whole new lifestyle to provide a healthy environment for your kidneys. For healthy kidneys, you just need to keep the following in mind:

Upgrade your vegetable intake to 5–9 vegetables per day.

Reduce the salt intake in your diet.

Cut down the overall protein intake.

Remove all the triggers of heart diseases, like fats and sugar, from your diet.

Do not consume pesticides and other environmental contaminants.

Try to consume fresh food; homemade is the best.

Avoid using food additives, as they contain high amounts of potassium, sodium, and phosphorous.

Drink lots of sodium-free drinks, especially water.

Choose to be more active and exercise regularly.

Do not smoke in order to avoid toxicity.

Obesity can create a greater risk of kidney diseases, so control your weight.

Do not take painkillers excessively, such as Ibuprofen, as they can also damage your kidneys.

PART 1: RECIPES FOR CHILDREN

Chapter 6: Breakfast for Children

Blackberry Pudding

Serving: 2

Preparation Time: 45 minutes

Cooking Time: Nil Ingredients:

¼ cup chia seeds

½ cup blackberries, fresh

1 teaspoon liquid sweetener

1 cup coconut milk, full fat and unsweetened

1 teaspoon vanilla extract

Direction:

Take the vanilla, liquid sweetener and coconut milk and add to blender

Process until thick

Add blackberries and process until smooth

Divide the mixture between cups and chill for 30 minutes

Serve and enjoy!

Nutrition (Per Serving)

Calories: 437

Fat: 38g

Carbohydrates: 8g

Protein: 8g

Simple Green Shake

Serving: 1

Preparation Time: 10 minutes

Ingredients:

¾ cup whole milk yogurt

2½ cups lettuce, mix salad greens

1 pack stevia

1 tablespoon MCT oil

1 tablespoon chia seeds

1 ½ cups of water

Direction: Add listed ingredients to a blender

Blend until you have a smooth and creamy texture

Serve chilled and enjoy!

Nutrition (Per Serving)

Calories: 320

Fat: 24g

Carbohydrates: 17g

Protein: 10g

Green Beans and Roasted Onion

Serving: 6

Preparation Time: 10 minutes

Cooking Time: 15 minutes

Ingredients:

1 yellow onion, sliced into rings

½ teaspoon onion powder

2 tablespoons coconut flour

1 1/3 pounds fresh green beans, trimmed and chopped

½ tablespoon salt

Direction:

Take a large bowl and mix the salt with the onion powder and coconut flour

Add onion rings

Mix well to coat

Spread the rings in the baking sheet, lined with parchment paper

Drizzle with some oil

Bake for 10 minutes at 400°F

Parboil the green beans for 3 to 5 minutes in the boiling water

Drain and serve the beans with the baked onion rings

Serve warm and enjoy!

Nutrition (Per Serving)

Calories: 214

Fat: 19.4g

Carbohydrates:3.7g

Protein: 8.3g

Fine Morning Porridge

Serving: 2

Preparation Time: 15 minutes

Cooking Time: Nil Ingredients:

2 tablespoons coconut flour

2 tablespoons vanilla protein powder

3 tablespoons Golden Flaxseed meal

1 ½ cups almond milk, unsweetened

Powdered erythritol

Direction: Take a bowl and mix in flaxseed meal, protein powder, coconut flour and mix well

Add mix to the saucepan (placed over medium heat)

Add almond milk and stir, let the mixture thicken

Add your desired amount of sweetener and serve

Nutrition (Per Serving)

Calories: 259

Fat: 13g

Carbohydrates: 5g

Protein: 16g

Hungarian's Porridge

Serving: 2

Preparation Time: 10 minutes

Cooking Time: 5-10 minutes

Ingredients:

1 tablespoon chia seeds

1 tablespoon ground flaxseed

1/3 cup coconut cream

½ cup of water

1 teaspoon vanilla extract

1 tablespoon almond butter

Direction:

Add chia seeds, coconut cream, flaxseed, water and vanilla to a small pot

Stir and let it sit for 5 minutes

Add butter and place pot over low heat

Keep stirring as butter melts

Once the porridge is hot/not boiling, pour into a bowl

Enjoy!

Add a few berries or a dash of cream for extra flavor

Nutrition (Per Serving)

Calories: 410

Fat: 38g

Carbohydrates: 10g

Protein: 6g

Awesome Nut Porridge

Serving: 4

Preparation Time: 10 minutes

Cooking Time: 15 minutes

Ingredients:

1 cup cashew nuts, raw and unsalted

1 cup pecan, halved

2 tablespoons stevia

4 teaspoons coconut oil, melted

2 cups of water

Direction:

Chop the nuts in a food processor and form a smooth paste

Add water, oil, stevia to the nut paste and transfer the mix to a saucepan

Stir cook for 5 minutes on high heat

Reduce heat to low and simmer for 10 minutes

Serve warm and enjoy!

Nutrition (Per Serving)

Calories: 260

Fat: 22g

Carbohydrates: 12g

Protein: 6g

Zucchini and Onion Platter

Serving: 4

Preparation Time: 15 minutes

Cooking Time: 45 minutes

Ingredients:

3 large zucchinis, julienned

½ cup basil

2 red onions, thinly sliced

¼ teaspoon salt

1 teaspoon cayenne pepper

2 tablespoons lemon juice

Direction:

Create zucchini Zoodles by using a vegetable peeler and shaving the zucchini with peeler lengthwise until you get to the core and seeds

Turn zucchini and repeat until you have long strips

Discard seeds

Lay strips on cutting board and slice lengthwise to your desired thickness

Mix Zoodles in a bowl alongside onion, basil, and toss

Sprinkle salt and cayenne pepper on top

Drizzle lemon juice

Serve and enjoy!

Nutrition (Per Serving)

Calories: 156

Fat: 8g

Carbohydrates: 6g

Protein: 7g

Onion Cheese Omelet

Cooking time: *12 minutes*

Servings: *2*

Ingredients:

3 eggs

1/4 cup liquid creamer

1 tablespoon water

Black pepper to taste

1 tablespoon butter

3/4 cup onion, sliced

1 large apple, peeled, cored, and sliced

2 tablespoons Cheddar cheese, grated

Direction:

Switch your gas oven to 400 degrees F to preheat.

Whisk the eggs with the liquid creamer, water, and black pepper in a suitable bowl.

Stir ¼ of the butter into an oven safe skillet and sauté the onion and apple slices.

After 5 minutes, pour in the egg mixture over the onions.

Sprinkle Cheddar cheese over the egg and bake for approximately 12 minutes.

Slice the omelet and serve.

Nutritional information per serving: *Calories 254*

Total Fat 15.1g Saturated Fat 7.2g Cholesterol 268mg Sodium 184mg Carbohydrate 20.7g Dietary Fiber 3.6g Sugars 14.6g Protein 10.9g Calcium 98mg Phosphorous 334mg Potassium 280mg

Morning Patties

Cooking time: 6 minutes

Servings: 6

Ingredients:

1 lb. fresh lean ground chicken

2 teaspoons ground sage

2 teaspoons granulated Swerve

1 teaspoon ground black pepper

½ teaspoon ground red pepper

1 teaspoon basil

Direction:

Mix the ground chicken with the sage, Swerve, black pepper, red pepper, and basil in a suitable bowl.

Take 2 tablespoons of this meat mixture and make a patty.

Grease a cooking pan with cooking spray and place it over moderate heat.

Add the patties to the pan and sear them for 2-3 minutes per side.

Serve with fresh bread (optional).

Nutritional information per serving: *Calories 115*

Total Fat 6.2g Saturated Fat 1.8g Cholesterol 65mg Sodium 46mg Carbohydrate 0.8g Dietary Fiber 0.2g Sugars 0.3g Protein 13.3g Calcium 10mg Phosphorous 200 mg Potassium 405mg

Mushroom Omelet

Cooking time: *10 minutes*

Servings: *2*

Ingredients:

2 tablespoons and 1 teaspoon olive oil

1 shallot, minced

¼ lb. cremini mushrooms, rinsed

Black pepper to taste

1 garlic clove, minced

2 teaspoons parsley, minced

4 eggs

1 tablespoon chives, minced

2 teaspoons milk

3 tablespoons Gruyere cheese, grated

Direction:

Set a suitable non-stick skillet over moderate heat and add 1 teaspoon olive oil.

Add in the shallot and mushrooms, then sauté for 5 minutes until soft.

Toss in the garlic and sauté for 1 minute.

Now add the rest of the oil to the same skillet.

Mix the eggs with the chives, milk, and black pepper in a bowl and pour it into the skillet.

Cook the egg omelet for about 2 minutes per side until golden brown then transfers to the serving place.

Serve with Gruyere cheese and parsley on top.

Enjoy.

Nutritional information per serving: *Calories 271*

Total Fat 23g Saturated Fat 4.8g Cholesterol 328mg Sodium 208mg Carbohydrate 4.8g Dietary Fiber 0.5g Sugars 2g Protein 13g Calcium 71mg Phosphorous 227mg Potassium 410mg

Chapter 7: Lunch for Children

Garlicky Balsamic Chicken

Cooking time: 30 minutes

Servings: 8

Ingredients:

2 cups low-sodium chicken broth

1/2 cup balsamic vinegar

1/2 cup white wine

1 tablespoon rosemary, chopped

8 chicken breasts, boneless, skinless

1 garlic head, chopped

2 tablespoons olive oil

Black pepper, to taste

Direction:

Begin by mixing the wine, rosemary, broth, and vinegar in a 9x13 inch baking pan.

Add the chicken breasts and rub well with the mixture. Marinate overnight.

Grease a saucepan with oil and add the garlic.

Sauté until golden, then keep the garlic aside.

Season the marinated chicken with black pepper and sear it for 5 minutes per side until golden.

Pour the reserved marinade over it along with the garlic.

Cook on reduced heat for 15 minutes and flip the chicken after 7 minutes.

Transfer the chicken to the serving plates.

Cook the remaining cooking liquid until it thickens.

Pour the sauce over the chicken.

Serve warm and fresh.

Nutritional information per serving: *Calories 265*

Total Fat 3.4g Saturated Fat 0.1g Cholesterol 130mg Sodium 188mg Carbohydrate 1.6g Dietary Fiber 0.3g Sugars 0.2g Protein 37.3g Calcium 11mg Phosphorous 221mg Potassium 34mg

Salisbury Meat Steak

Cooking time: *25 minutes*

Servings: *4*

Ingredients:

1 lb. steak, finely chopped

1 small onion, chopped

½ cup green pepper, chopped

1 teaspoon black pepper

1 egg

1 tablespoon olive oil

½ cup water

1 tablespoon corn starch

Direction:

Mix the steak with the green pepper, egg, black pepper and onion in a bowl.

Add the oil to a skillet and place the patties in.

Sear the steak patties for 5 minutes per side until golden brown.

Add half of the water and let the patties simmer for 15 minutes.

Whisk the remaining water with cornstarch in a bowl.

Add this cornstarch mixture to the patties and cook until the sauce thickens.

Serve warm.

Nutritional information per serving: *Calories 276*

Total Fat 11.6g Saturated Fat 3.7g Cholesterol 142mg Sodium 92mg Carbohydrate 4.8g Dietary Fiber 0.7g Sugars 1.1g Protein 33.1g Calcium 16mg Phosphorous 361mg Potassium 524mg.

Eggplant Fries

Preparation Time: 10 minutes

Cooking Time: 5 minutes

Servings: 6

Ingredients:

2 eggs, beaten

1 cup almond milk

1 teaspoon hot sauce

3/4 cup cornstarch

3 teaspoons dry ranch seasoning mix

3/4 cup dry bread crumbs

1 eggplant, sliced into strips

1/2 cup oil

Direction:

In a bowl, mix eggs, milk and hot sauce.

In a dish, mix cornstarch, seasoning and breadcrumbs.

Dip first the eggplant strips in the egg mixture.

Coat each strip with the cornstarch mixture.

Pour oil in a pan over medium heat.

Once hot, add the fries and cook for 3 minutes or until golden.

Nutrition:

Calories 233

Protein 5 g

Carbohydrates 24 g

Fat 13 g

Cholesterol 48 mg

Sodium 212 mg

Potassium 215 mg

Phosphorus 86 mg

Calcium 70 mg

Fiber 2.1 g

Seasoned Green Beans

Preparation Time: 10 minutes

Cooking Time: 10 minutes

Servings: 4

Ingredients:

10 oz. green beans

4 teaspoons butter

1/4 cup onion, chopped

1/2 cup red bell pepper, chopped

1 teaspoon dried dill weed

1 teaspoon dried parsley

1/4 teaspoon black pepper

Direction:

Boil green beans in a pot of water. Drain.

In a pan over medium heat, melt the butter and cook onion and bell pepper.

Season with dill and parsley.

Put the green beans back to the skillet.

Sprinkle pepper on top before serving.

Nutrition:

Calories 67

Protein 2 g

Carbohydrates 8 g

Fat 3 g

Cholesterol 0 mg

Sodium 55 mg

Potassium 194 mg

Phosphorus 32 mg

Calcium 68 mg

Fiber 4.0 g

Grilled Squash

Preparation Time: 10 minutes

Cooking Time: 6 minutes

Servings: 8

Ingredients:

4 zucchinis, rinsed, drained and sliced

4 crookneck squash, rinsed, drained and sliced

Cooking spray

1/4 teaspoon garlic powder

1/4 teaspoon black pepper

Direction:

Arrange squash on a baking sheet.

Spray with oil.

Season with garlic powder and pepper.

Grill for 3 minutes per side or until tender but not too soft.

Nutrition:

Calories 17

Protein 1 g

Carbohydrates 3 g

Fat 0 g

Cholesterol 0 mg

Sodium 6 mg

Potassium 262 mg

Phosphorus 39 mg

Calcium 16 mg

Fiber 1.1 g

Vegetable Medley

Preparation Time: 3 hours and 15 minutes

Cooking Time: 0 minutes

Servings: 12

Ingredients:

1 cup celery, chopped

2 cups mushrooms, sliced

1 cup green bell pepper, sliced

3 cups cauliflower florets, steamed and sliced

3 cups broccoli florets, steamed sliced

1 cup olive oil

½ cup onion, chopped

2 teaspoons dry mustard

½ cup sugar

½ cup vinegar

1 tablespoon poppy seeds

Direction:

In a bowl, combine celery, mushrooms, bell pepper, cauliflower and broccoli.

In another bowl, mix the rest of the ingredients.

Marinate vegetables in the mixture for 3 hours in the refrigerator.

Remove from marinade before serving.

Nutrition:

Calories 174

Protein 2 g

Carbohydrates 10 g

Fat 14 g

Cholesterol 0 mg

Sodium 95 mg

Potassium 250 mg

Phosphorus 50 mg

Calcium 33 mg

Fiber 1.9 g

Sausage & Egg Soup

Preparation Time: 15 minutes

Cooking Time: 30 minutes

Servings: 4

Ingredients:

½ lb. ground beef

Black pepper

½ teaspoon ground sage

½ teaspoon garlic powder

½ teaspoon dried basil

4 slices bread (one day old), cubed

2 tablespoons olive oil

1 tablespoon herb seasoning blend

2 garlic cloves, minced

3 cups low-sodium chicken broth

1 cup water

4 tablespoons fresh parsley

4 eggs

2 tablespoons Parmesan cheese, grated

Direction:

Preheat your oven to 375 degrees F.

Mix the first five ingredients to make the sausage.

Toss bread cubes in oil and seasoning blend.

Bake in the oven for 8 minutes. Set aside.

Cook the sausage in a pan over medium heat.

Cook the garlic in the sausage drippings for 2 minutes.

Stir in the broth, water and parsley.

Bring to a boil and then simmer for 10 minutes.

Pour into serving bowls and top with baked bread, egg and sausage.

Nutrition:

Calories 335

Protein 26 g

Carbohydrates 15 g

Fat 19 g

Cholesterol 250 mg

Sodium 374 mg

Potassium 392 mg

Phosphorus 268 mg

Calcium 118 mg

Fiber 0.9 g

Spring Veggie Soup

Preparation Time: 20 minutes

Cooking Time: 45 minutes

Servings: 5

Ingredients:

2 tablespoons olive oil

½ cup onion, diced

½ cup mushrooms, sliced

1/8 cup celery, chopped

1 tomato, diced

½ cup carrots, diced

1 cup green beans, trimmed

½ cup frozen corn

1 teaspoon garlic powder

1 teaspoon dried oregano leaves

4 cups low-sodium vegetable broth

Direction:

In a pot, pour the olive oil and cook the onion and celery for 2 minutes.

Add the rest of the ingredients.

Bring to a boil.

Reduce heat and simmer for 45 minutes.

Nutrition:

Calories 114

Protein 2 g

Carbohydrates 13 g

Fat 6 g

Cholesterol 0 mg

Sodium 262 mg

Potassium 400 mg

Phosphorus 108 mg

Calcium 48 mg

Fiber 3.4 g

Seafood Chowder with Corn

Preparation Time: 15 minutes

Cooking Time: 20 minutes

Servings: 10

Ingredients:

1 tablespoon butter (unsalted)

1 cup onion, chopped

1/2 cup red bell pepper, chopped

1/2 cup green bell pepper, chopped

1/4 cup celery, chopped

1 tablespoon all-purpose white flour

14 oz. low-sodium chicken broth

2 cups nondairy creamer

6 oz. almond milk

10 oz. crab flakes

2 cups corn kernels

1/2 teaspoon paprika

Black pepper to taste

Direction:

In a pan over medium heat, melt the butter and cook the onion, bell peppers and celery for 4 minutes.

Stir in the flour and cook for 2 minutes.

Add the broth and bring to a boil.

Add the rest of the ingredients.

Stir occasionally, and cook for 5 minutes.

Nutrition:

Calories 173

Protein 8 g

Carbohydrates 22 g

Fat 7 g

Cholesterol 13 mg

Sodium 160 mg

Potassium 285 mg

Phosphorus 181 mg

Calcium 68 mg

Fiber 1.5 g

Taco Soup

Preparation Time: 30 minutes

Cooking Time: 7 hours

Servings: 10

Ingredients:

1 lb. chicken breast (boneless, skinless)

15 oz. canned red kidney beans, rinsed and drained

15 oz. low-sodium white corn, rinsed and drained

15 oz. canned yellow hominy, rinsed and drained

1 cup canned diced tomatoes with green chilies

1/2 cup onion, chopped

1/2 cup green bell peppers, chopped

1 clove garlic, chopped

1 jalapeno, chopped

1 tablespoon low-sodium taco seasoning

2 cups low-sodium chicken broth

Direction:

Put chicken in the slow cooker.

Top with the rest of the ingredients.

Cook on high for 1 hour.

Set to low and cook for 6 hours.

Shred chicken and serve with the soup.

Nutrition:

Calories 190

Protein 21 g

Carbohydrates 19 g

Fat 3 g

Cholesterol 42 mg

Sodium 421 mg

Potassium 444 mg

Phosphorus 210 mg

Calcium 28 mg

Fiber 4.3 g

Rice with stir-fried chicken fillet and bok choy

Cooking time: 30 minutes

Servings: 8

Ingredients

200 g chicken fillet

1 shrub bok choy

1 red pepper

200 g of rice

2 tbsp oil

2 tbsp curry

1 clove of garlic, chopped

½ red pepper, chopped without seeds

1 cup of crème Fraiche

Direction

Cut the chicken into cubes. Clean the bok choy and cut the stems and leaves into strips of approximately 2 centimeters. Clean the bell pepper and cut it into small strips.

Prepare the rice according to the Direction on the package. In the meantime, heat the oil in a wok (or frying pan) and stir-fry the chicken until brown, then fry the garlic and chilli.

Sprinkle the chicken with the curry and stir in the bok choy and bell pepper. Stir fry the whole for another 5 minutes.

Drain the rice well. Stir the crème fraîche into the meat and vegetable mixture and stir-fry until everything is thoroughly hot. Season the dish with pepper.

Nutrition:

Calories 114

Protein 2 g

Carbohydrates 13 g

Fat 6 g

Cholesterol 0 mg

Sodium 262 mg

Potassium 400 mg

Phosphorus 108 mg

Calcium 48 mg

Fiber 3.4 g

Pasta with avocado pesto and broccoli

Cooking time: 30 minutes

Servings: 8

Ingredients

200 g (whole grain) pasta

300 g broccoli florets

1 lemon, waxed

1 avocado

1 large hand fresh basil (approx. 20 g)

2 cloves of garlic...

25 g pine nuts

30 g grated Parmesan cheese

freshly ground pepper

2 tbsp olive oil

Requirements: food processor or hand blender

Direction

Cook the pasta according to the Direction on the package. When draining the pasta, save ¼ cup of water for the pesto. Cook the broccoli florets in about 8 minutes until done.

Grate half a zest of the lemon and squeeze the fruit. Cut the avocado in half, remove the kernel and cut into strips. Spoon the strips out of the peel.

In a food processor, add the basil, garlic, pine nuts, Parmesan cheese, zest of half lemon, juice of whole lemon and some freshly ground pepper. Mix everything well and gradually add the olive oil while mixing and mix until smooth. Then add the avocado and the remaining pasta water. Mix everything well again.

Add the sauce to the cooked pasta and stir well so that it is completely covered with the sauce. Finally add the broccoli to the pasta and serve.

Nutrition:

Calories 114

Protein 2 g

Carbohydrates 13 g

Fat 6 g

Cholesterol 0 mg

Sodium 262 mg

Potassium 400 mg

Phosphorus 108 mg

Calcium 48 mg

Fiber 3.4 g

Fish package with cod

Cooking time: 30 minutes

Servings: 8

Ingredients

400 g of rice

4 sheets of aluminum foil

dash of oil

dash of coconut milk

400 g zucchini

400 g fennel

4 pieces of cod of approximately 100 grams

2 tbsp dill

2 lemons

black pepper or 4-season pepper

Direction

Heat the oven to 180 ° C.

Cook the rice according to the Direction on the package.

Cut the zucchini into cubes and the fennel into slices.

Put the aluminum foil down and spread the rice over it with some oil and coconut milk. Place the zucchini and fennel on top and then place the cod on the rice and vegetables. Divide the dill over the packages.

Squeeze one of the lemons and cut the other into segments. Divide the juice and the segments over the packages. Add pepper to taste.

Fold the packages tightly. (No steam may escape.) Place the packets in the oven for 20-25 minutes (depending on the thickness of the fish).

Nutrition:

Calories 114

Protein 2 g

Carbohydrates 13 g

Fat 6 g

Cholesterol 0 mg

Sodium 262 mg

Potassium 400 mg

Phosphorus 108 mg

Calcium 48 mg

Fiber 3.4 g

Spaghetti with kale and meatballs

Cooking time: 30 minutes

Servings: 8

Ingredients

350 g half-to-half minced meat

300 g sliced kale

1 rusk

1 tbsp dried oregano

2 tsp Jonnie Boer Picadillo (spice mix)

250 g mushrooms in pieces

2 tbsp liquid fry & roast

freshly ground pepper

1 onion, chopped

300 g (whole grain) spaghetti

2 cloves of garlic, chopped

piece of Parmesan cheese

4 sun-dried tomatoes (in oil) in pieces

Direction

Put the minced meat in a bowl, crumble the rusk above it and sprinkle with the spice mix. Knead well together and make small meatballs.

Heat the frying pan in a frying pan with a small dash of oil (from the sun-dried tomatoes). Bake the meatballs brown, add a splash of water and cook for about 10 minutes with the lid on the pan. Keep warm with a lid on the pan.

Bring a pan of water to the boil for the spaghetti (add the spaghetti later).

Heat 2 tablespoons of oil in a wok and fry the onion until it is glassy, then add the garlic and the tomato pieces and fry for 1 minute. Add the kale and stir until it has shrunk. Add a tablespoon of boiling water. Put a lid on the pan and let it simmer for 20 minutes. Add the oregano after 15 minutes.

In another frying pan, heat a tablespoon of oil and add the mushrooms with freshly ground pepper. Allow the moisture to evaporate and then bake until golden brown, stirring.

Cook the spaghetti at the same time.

Spoon the spaghetti and mushrooms into the wok and mix in the kale.

Serve the spaghetti with the minced meat balls. Grate some Parmesan cheese on the plate.

Nutrition:

Calories 114

Protein 2 g

Carbohydrates 13 g

Fat 6 g

Cholesterol 0 mg

Sodium 262 mg

Potassium 400 mg

Phosphorus 108 mg

Calcium 48 mg

Fiber 3.4 g

Couscous with pumpkin and chickpeas

Cooking time: 30 minutes

Servings: 8

Ingredients

1 bottle squash

1 tbsp liquid frying fat

2 tbsp honey

200 g couscous

1 orange, waxed

400 g canned chickpeas...

4 tbsp olive oil

2 tsp ras el hanout (for example from Jonnie de Boer or Pure Spices from firm Verstegen)

75 g raisins

Direction

Preheat the oven to 200 ° C.

Wash the pumpkin and halve the length. Remove the seeds and stringy inside with a spoon. Leave the skin on. Cut both halves into 1 cm cubes.

Grease the baking sheet with liquid baking & roasting (or use baking paper).

Mix the pumpkin with the honey and spread on the greased baking sheet.

Bake the pumpkin in the oven for about 20 minutes until the pumpkin is cooked. Scoop halfway through once.

Meanwhile, prepare the couscous according to the Direction on the package.

Grate the orange zest of the orange and squeeze the fruit.

Drain the chickpeas in a colander and rinse with cold running water. Mix the couscous with orange zest and juice, chickpeas, olive oil, ras el hanout and raisins.

Divide the pumpkin on the couscous.

Nutrition:

Calories 114

Protein 2 g

Carbohydrates 13 g

Fat 6 g

Cholesterol 0 mg

Sodium 262 mg

Potassium 400 mg

Phosphorus 108 mg

Calcium 48 mg

Fiber 3.4 g

Chapter 8: Dinner for Children

Lemon Butter Salmon

Preparation Time: 15 minutes

Cooking Time: 15 minutes

Servings: 6

Ingredients:

1 tablespoon butter

2 tablespoons olive oil

1 tablespoon Dijon mustard

1 tablespoons lemon juice

2 cloves garlic, crushed

1 teaspoon dried dill

1 teaspoon dried basil leaves

1 tablespoon capers

24 oz. salmon filet

Direction:

Put all the ingredients except the salmon in a saucepan over medium heat.

Bring to a boil and then simmer for 5 minutes.

Preheat your grill.

Create a packet using foil.

Place the sauce and salmon inside.

Seal the packet.

Grill for 12 minutes.

Nutrition:

Calories 294

Protein 23 g

Carbohydrates 1 g

Fat 22 g

Cholesterol 68 mg

Sodium 190 mg

Potassium 439 mg

Phosphorus 280 mg

Calcium 21 mg

Crab Cake

Preparation Time: 15 minutes

Cooking Time: 9 minutes

Servings: 6

Ingredients:

1/4 cup onion, chopped

1/4 cup bell pepper, chopped

1 egg, beaten

6 low-sodium crackers, crushed

1/4 cup low-fat mayonnaise

1 lb. crab meat

1 tablespoon dry mustard

Pepper to taste

2 tablespoons lemon juice

1 tablespoon fresh parsley

1 tablespoon garlic powder

3 tablespoons olive oil

Direction:

Mix all the ingredients except the oil.

Form 6 patties from the mixture.

Pour the oil into a pan over medium heat.

Cook the crab cakes for 5 minutes.

Flip and cook for another 4 minutes.

Nutrition:

Calories 188

Protein 13 g

Carbohydrates 5 g

Fat 13 g

Cholesterol 111 mg

Sodium 342 mg

Potassium 317 mg

Phosphorus 185 mg

Calcium 52 mg

Fiber 0.5 g

Baked Fish in Cream Sauce

Preparation Time: 10 minutes

Cooking Time: 40 minutes

Servings: 4

Ingredients:

1 lb. haddock

1/2 cup all-purpose flour

2 tablespoons butter (unsalted)

1/4 teaspoon pepper

2 cups fat-free nondairy creamer

1/4 cup water

Direction:

Preheat your oven to 350 degrees F.

Spray baking pan with oil.

Sprinkle with a little flour.

Arrange fish on the pan

Season with pepper.

Sprinkle remaining flour on the fish.

Spread creamer on both sides of the fish.

Bake for 40 minutes or until golden.

Spread cream sauce on top of the fish before serving.

Nutrition:

Calories 380

Protein 23 g

Carbohydrates 46 g

Fat 11 g

Cholesterol 79 mg

Sodium 253 mg

Potassium 400 mg

Phosphorus 266 mg

Calcium 46 mg

Fiber 0.4 g

Parsley Scallops

Serving: 4

Preparation Time: 5 minutes

Cooking Time: 25 minutes

Ingredients:

8 tablespoons almond butter

2 garlic cloves, minced

16 large sea scallops

Salt and pepper to taste

1 ½ tablespoons olive oil

Direction:

Seasons scallops with salt and pepper

Take a skillet and place it over medium heat, add oil and let it heat up

Sauté scallops for 2 minutes per side, repeat until all scallops are cooked

Add butter to the skillet and let it melt

Stir in garlic and cook for 15 minutes

Return scallops to skillet and stir to coat

Serve and enjoy!

Nutrition (Per Serving)

Calories: 417

Fat: 31g

Net Carbohydrates: 5g

Protein: 29g

Blackened Chicken

Serving: 4

Preparation Time: 10 minutes

Cooking Time: 10 minutes

Ingredients:

½ teaspoon paprika

1/8 teaspoon salt

¼ teaspoon cayenne pepper

¼ teaspoon ground cumin

¼ teaspoon dried thyme

1/8 teaspoon ground white pepper

1/8 teaspoon onion powder

2 chicken breasts, boneless and skinless

Direction:

Preheat your oven to 350 °F

Grease baking sheet

Take a cast-iron skillet and place it over high heat

Add oil and heat it up for 5 minutes until smoking hot

Take a small bowl and mix salt, paprika, cumin, white pepper, cayenne, thyme, onion powder

Oil the chicken breast on both sides and coat the breast with the spice mix

Transfer to your hot pan and cook for 1 minute per side

Transfer to your prepared baking sheet and bake for 5 minutes

Serve and enjoy!

Nutrition (Per Serving)

Calories: 136

Fat: 3g

Carbohydrates: 1g

Protein: 24g

Spicy Paprika Lamb Chops

Serving: 4

Preparation Time: 10 minutes

Cooking Time: 15 minutes

Ingredients:

2 lamb racks, cut into chops

Salt and pepper to taste

3 tablespoons paprika

¾ cup cumin powder

1 teaspoon chili powder

Direction:

Take a bowl and add the paprika, cumin, chili, salt, pepper, and stir

Add lamb chops and rub the mixture

Heat grill over medium-temperature and add lamb chops, cook for 5 minutes

Flip and cook for 5 minutes more, flip again

Cook for 2 minutes, flip and cook for 2 minutes more

Serve and enjoy!

Nutrition (Per Serving)

Calories: 200

Fat: 5g

Carbohydrates: 4g

Protein: 8g

One-Pot Beef Roast

Serving: 4

Preparation Time: 10 minutes

Cooking Time: 75 minutes

Ingredients:

3 ½ pounds beef roast

4 ounces mushrooms, sliced

12 ounces beef stock

1-ounce onion soup mix

½ cup Italian dressing

Direction:

Take a bowl and add the stock, onion soup mix, and Italian dressing

Stir

Put beef roast in pan

Add the mushrooms and stock mix to the pan and cover with foil

Preheat your oven to 300 °F

Bake for 1 hour and 15 minutes

Let the roast cool

Slice and serve

Enjoy the gravy on top!

Nutrition (Per Serving)

Calories: 700

Fat: 56g

Carbohydrates: 10g

Protein: 70g

Cabbage and Beef Fry

Serving: 4

Preparation Time: 5 minutes
Cooking Time: 15 minutes
Ingredients:

1-pound beef, ground

½ pound bacon

1 onion

1 garlic clove, minced

½ head cabbage

Salt and pepper to taste

Direction:

Take a skillet and place it over medium heat

Add chopped bacon, beef and onion until slightly browned

Transfer to a bowl and keep it covered

Add minced garlic and cabbage to the skillet and cook until slightly browned

Return the ground beef mixture to the skillet and simmer for 3-5 minutes over low heat

Serve and enjoy!

Nutrition (Per Serving)

Calories: 360

Fat: 22g

Net Carbohydrates: 5g

Protein: 34g

Mushroom and Olive Sirloin Steak

Serving: 4

Preparation Time: 10 minutes

Cooking Time: 14 minutes

Ingredients:

1-pound boneless beef sirloin steak, ¾ inch thick, cut into 4 pieces

1 large red onion, chopped

1 cup mushrooms

4 garlic cloves, thinly sliced

4 tablespoons olive oil

½ cup green olives, coarsely chopped

1 cup parsley leaves, finely cut

Direction:

Take a large-sized skillet and place it over medium-high heat

Add oil and let it heat p

Add beef and cook until both sides are browned, remove beef and drain fat

Add the rest of the oil to skillet and heat it up

Add onions, garlic and cook for 2-3 minutes

Stir well

Add mushrooms olives and cook until mushrooms are thoroughly done

Return beef to skillet and lower heat to medium

Cook for 3-4 minutes (covered)

Stir in parsley

Serve and enjoy!

Nutrition (Per Serving)

Calories: 386

Fat: 30g

Carbohydrates: 11g

Protein: 21g

Parsley and Chicken Breast

Serving: 4

Preparation Time: 10 minutes

Cooking Time: 40 minutes

Ingredients:

1 tablespoon dry parsley

1 tablespoon dry basil

4 chicken breast halves, boneless and skinless

½ teaspoon salt

½ teaspoon red pepper flakes, crushed

Direction:

Preheat your oven to 350 °F

Take a 9x13 inch baking dish and grease it with cooking spray

Sprinkle 1 tablespoon of parsley, 1 teaspoon of basil and spread the mixture over your baking dish

Arrange the chicken breast halves over the dish and sprinkle garlic slices on top

Take a small bowl and add 1 teaspoon parsley, 1 teaspoon of basil, salt, basil, red pepper and mix well. Pour the mixture over the chicken breast

Bake for 25 minutes

Remove the cover and bake for 15 minutes more

Serve and enjoy!

Nutrition (Per Serving)

Calories: 150

Fat: 4g

Carbohydrates: 4g

Protein: 25g

Saucy Dill Fish

Cooking time: *15 minutes*

Servings: *4*

Ingredients:

4 (4 oz.) salmon fillets

Dill Sauce:

1 cup whipped cream cheese

4 minced garlic cloves

½ small onion, diced

3 tablespoons fresh or dried dill (as desired)

½ teaspoon ground pepper

1 teaspoon Mrs. Dash (optional)

2 drops of hot sauce (optional)

Direction:

Place the salmon fillets in a moderately shallow baking stray.

Whisk the cream cheese and all the dill-sauce ingredients in a bowl.

Spread the dill-sauce over the fillets liberally.

Cover the fillet pan with a foil sheet and bake for 15 minutes at 350 degrees F.

Serve warm.

Nutritional information per serving: *Calories 432*

Total Fat 26.7g Saturated Fat 12.9g Cholesterol 142mg Sodium 280mg Carbohydrate 5g Dietary Fiber 0.9g Sugars 2.25g Protein 35.8g Calcium 141mg Phosphorous 265mg Potassium 590mg

Chapter 9: Desserts for Children

The Coconut Loaf

Serving: 4

Preparation Time: 15 minutes

Cooking Time: 40 minutes

Ingredients:

1 ½ tablespoons coconut flour

¼ teaspoon on baking powder

1/8 teaspoon salt

1 tablespoon coconut oil, melted

1 whole egg

Direction:

Preheat your oven to 350 °F

Add coconut flour, baking powder, salt

Add coconut oil, eggs and stir well until mixed

Leave the batter for several minutes

Pour half the batter onto the baking pan

Spread it to form a circle, repeat with remaining batter

Bake in the oven for 10 minutes

Once a golden-brown texture comes, let it cool and serve

Enjoy!

Nutrition (Per Serving)

Calories: 297

Fat: 14g

Carbohydrates: 15g

Protein: 15g

Chocolate Parfait

Serving: 4

Preparation Time: 2 hours Cook Time: nil Ingredients:

2 tablespoons cocoa powder

1 cup almond milk

1 tablespoon chia seeds

Pinch of salt

½ teaspoon vanilla extract

Direction:

Take a bowl and add cocoa powder, almond milk, chia seeds, vanilla extract, and stir

Transfer to dessert glass and place in your fridge for 2 hours

Serve and enjoy!

Nutrition (Per Serving)

Calories: 130

Fat: 5g

Carbohydrates: 7g

Protein: 16g

Cauliflower Bagel

Serving: 12

Preparation Time: 10 minutes

Cooking Time: 30 minutes

Ingredients:

1 large cauliflower, divided into florets and roughly chopped

¼ cup nutritional yeast

¼ cup almond flour

½ teaspoon garlic powder

1 ½ teaspoon fine sea salt

2 whole eggs

1 tablespoon sesame seeds

Direction:

Preheat your oven to 400 °F

Line a baking sheet with parchment paper, keep it on the side

Blend cauliflower in a food processor and transfer to a bowl

Add nutritional yeast, almond flour, garlic powder and salt to a bowl, mix

Take another bowl and whisk in eggs, add to cauliflower mix

Give the dough a stir

Incorporate the mix into the egg mix

Make balls from the dough, making a hole using your thumb into each ball

Arrange them on your prepped sheet, flattening them into bagel shapes

Sprinkle sesame seeds and bake for half an hour

Remove the oven and let them cool, enjoy!

Nutrition (Per Serving)

Calories: 152

Fat: 10g

Carbohydrates: 4g

Protein: 4g

Lemon Mousse

Serving: 4

Preparation Time: 10 + chill time Cook Time: 10 minutes

Ingredients:

1 cup coconut cream

8 ounces cream cheese, soft

¼ cup fresh lemon juice

3 pinches salt

1 teaspoon lemon liquid stevia

Direction:

Preheat your oven to 350 °F

Grease a ramekin with butter

Beat cream, cream cheese, fresh lemon juice, salt and lemon liquid stevia in a mixer

Pour batter into ramekin

Bake for 10 minutes, then transfer the mousse to a serving glass

Let it chill for 2 hours and serve

Enjoy!

Nutrition (Per Serving)

Calories: 395

Fat: 31g

Carbohydrates: 3g

Protein: 5g

Jalapeno Crisp

Serving: 20

Preparation Time: 10 minutes

Cooking Time: 1 hour 15 minutes

Ingredients:

1 cup sesame seeds

1 cup sunflower seeds

1 cup flaxseeds

½ cup hulled hemp seeds

3 tablespoons Psyllium husk

1 teaspoon salt

1 teaspoon baking powder

2 cups of water

Direction:

Preheat your oven to 350 °F

Take your blender and add seeds, baking powder, salt, and Psyllium husk

Blend well until a sand-like texture appears

Stir in water and mix until a batter form

Allow the batter to rest for 10 minutes until a dough-like thick mixture forms

Pour the dough onto a cookie sheet lined with parchment paper

Spread it evenly, making sure that it has a thickness of ¼ inch thick all around

Bake for 75 minutes in your oven

Remove and cut into 20 spices

Allow them to cool for 30 minutes and enjoy!

Nutrition (Per Serving)

Calories: 156

Fat: 13g

Carbohydrates: 2g

Protein: 5g

Raspberry Popsicle

Serving: 4

Preparation Time: 2 hours Cook Time: 15 minutes

Ingredients:

1 ½ cups raspberries

2 cups of water

Direction: Take a pan and fill it up with water

Add raspberries

Place it over medium heat and bring to water to a boil

Reduce the heat and simmer for 15 minutes

Remove heat and pour the mix into Popsicle molds

Add a popsicle stick and let it chill for 2 hours

Nutrition (Per Serving)

Calories: 58

Fat: 0.4g

Carbohydrates: 0g

Protein: 1.4g

Easy Fudge

Serving: 25

Preparation Time: 15 minutes + chill time Cook Time: 5 minutes

Ingredients:

1 ¾ cups of coconut butter

1 cup pumpkin puree

1 teaspoon ground cinnamon

¼ teaspoon ground nutmeg

1 tablespoon coconut oil

Direction:

Take an 8x8 inch square baking pan and line it with aluminum foil

Take a spoon and scoop out the coconut butter into a heated pan and allow the butter to melt

Keep stirring well and remove from the heat once fully melted

Add spices and pumpkin and keep straining until you have a grain-like texture

Add coconut oil and keep stirring to incorporate everything

Scoop the mixture into your baking pan and evenly distribute it

Place wax paper on top of the mixture and press gently to straighten the top

Remove the paper and discard

Allow it to chill for 1-2 hours

Once chilled, take it out and slice it up into pieces

Enjoy!

Nutrition (Per Serving)

Calories: 120

Fat: 10g

Carbohydrates: 5g

Protein: 1.2g

Cashew and Almond Butter

Serving: 1 ½ cups Preparation Time: 5 minutes

Ingredients:

1 cup almonds, blanched

1/3 cup cashew nuts

2 tablespoons coconut oil

Salt as needed

½ teaspoon cinnamon

Direction:

Preheat your oven to 350 °F

Bake almonds and cashews for 12 minutes

Let them cool

Transfer to a food processor and add remaining ingredients

Add oil and keep blending until smooth

Serve and enjoy!

Nutrition (Per Serving)

Calories: 205

Fat: 19g

Carbohydrates: g

Protein: 2.8g

PART 2: RECIPES FOR ALL THE PEOPLE WITH THESE PROBLEMS

Chapter 10: Breakfast Recipes for the People with Kidney Problems

Cottage Cheese Pancakes

Cooking time: *10 minutes*

Servings: *4*

Ingredients:

1 cup cottage cheese

1/3 cup all-purpose flour

2 tablespoons vegetable oil

3 eggs, lightly beaten

Direction:

Begin by beating the eggs in a suitable bowl then stir in the cottage cheese.

Once it is well mixed, stir in the flour.

Pour a teaspoon of vegetable oil in a non-stick griddle and heat it.

Add ¼ cup of the batter in the griddle and cook for 2 minutes per side until brown.

Cook more of the pancakes using the remaining batter.

Serve.

Nutritional information per serving: *Calories 196*

Total Fat 11.3g Saturated Fat 3.1g Cholesterol 127mg Sodium 276mg Carbohydrate 10.3g Dietary Fiber 0.3g Sugars 0.5g Protein 13g Calcium 58mg Phosphorous 187 mg Potassium 110mg

Asparagus Bacon Hash

Cooking time: 27 minutes

Servings: 4

Ingredients:

6 slices bacon, diced

1/2 onion, chopped

2 cloves garlic, sliced

2 lb. asparagus, trimmed and chopped

Black pepper, to taste

2 tablespoons Parmesan, grated

4 large eggs

1/4 teaspoon red pepper flakes

Direction:

Add the asparagus and a tablespoon of water to a microwave proof bowl.

Cover the veggies and microwave them for 5 minutes until tender.

Set a suitable non-stick skillet over moderate heat and layer it with cooking spray.

Stir in the onion and sauté for 7 minutes, then toss in the garlic.

Stir for 1 minute, then toss in the asparagus, eggs, and red pepper flakes.

Reduce the heat to low and cover the vegetables in the pan. Top the eggs with Parmesan cheese.

Cook for approximately 15 minutes, then slice to serve.

Nutritional information per serving: *Calories 290*

Total Fat 17.9g Saturated Fat 6.1g Cholesterol 220mg Sodium 256mg Carbohydrate 11.6g Dietary Fiber 5.1g Sugars 5.3g Protein 23.2g Calcium 121mg Phosphorous 247mg Potassium 715mg

Cheese Spaghetti Frittata

Cooking time: *10 minutes*

Servings: 6

Ingredients:

4 cups whole-wheat spaghetti, cooked

4 teaspoons olive oil

3 medium onions, chopped

4 large eggs

½ cup milk

⅓ cup Parmesan cheese, grated

2 tablespoons fresh parsley, chopped

2 tablespoons fresh basil, chopped

½ teaspoon black pepper

1 tomato, diced

Direction:

Set a suitable non-stick skillet over moderate heat and add in the olive oil.

Place the spaghetti in the skillet and cook by stirring for 2 minutes on moderate heat.

Whisk the eggs with milk, parsley, and black pepper in a bowl.

Pour this milky egg mixture over the spaghetti and top it all with basil, cheese, and tomato.

Cover the spaghetti frittata again with a lid and cook for approximately 8 minutes on low heat.

Slice and serve.

Nutritional information per serving: *Calories 230*

Total Fat 7.8g Saturated Fat 2g Cholesterol 127mg Sodium 77mg Carbohydrate 31.9g Dietary Fiber 5.6g Sugars 4.5g Protein 11.1g Calcium 88mg Phosphorous 368 mg Potassium 214mg

Pineapple Bread

Cooking time: *1-hour* Servings: *10*

Ingredients:

1/3 cup Swerve

1/3 cup butter, unsalted

2 eggs

2 cups flour

3 teaspoons baking powder

1 cup pineapple, undrained

6 cherries, chopped

Direction:

Whisk the Swerve with the butter in a mixer until fluffy.

Stir in the eggs, then beat again.

Add the baking powder and flour, then mix well until smooth.

Fold in the cherries and pineapple.

Spread this cherry-pineapple batter in a 9x5 inch baking pan.

Bake the pineapple batter for 1 hour at 350 degrees F.

Slice the bread and serve.

Nutritional information per serving: *Calories 197*

Total Fat 7.2g Saturated Fat 1.3g Cholesterol 33mg Sodium 85mg Carbohydrate 18.3g Dietary Fiber 1.1g Sugars 3 g Protein 4g Calcium 79mg Phosphorous 316mg Potassium 227mg

Parmesan Zucchini Frittata

Cooking time: 35 minutes

Servings: 6

Ingredients:

1 tablespoon olive oil

1 cup yellow onion, sliced

3 cups zucchini, chopped

½ cup Parmesan cheese, grated

8 large eggs

½ teaspoon black pepper

⅛ teaspoon paprika

3 tablespoons parsley, chopped

Direction:

Toss the zucchinis with the onion, parsley, and all other ingredients in a large bowl.

Pour this zucchini-garlic mixture in an 11x7 inches pan and spread it evenly.

Bake the zucchini casserole for approximately 35 minutes at 350 degrees F.

Cut in slices and serve.

Nutritional information per serving: *Calories 142*

Total Fat 9.7g Saturated Fat 2.8g Cholesterol 250mg Sodium 123mg Carbohydrate 4.7g Dietary Fiber 1.3g Sugars 2.4g Protein 10.2g Calcium 73mg Phosphorous 375mg Potassium 286mg

Texas Toast Casserole

Cooking time: *30 minutes*

Servings: *10*

Ingredients:

1/2 cup butter, melted

1 cup brown Swerve

1 lb. Texas Toast bread, sliced

4 large eggs

1 1/2 cup milk

1 tablespoon vanilla extract

2 tablespoons Swerve

2 teaspoons cinnamon

Maple syrup for serving

Direction:

Layer a 9x13 inches baking pan with cooking spray.

Spread the bread slices at the bottom of the prepared pan.

Whisk the eggs with the remaining ingredients in a mixer.

Pour this mixture over the bread slices evenly.

Bake the bread for 30 minutes at 350 degrees F in a preheated oven.

Serve.

Nutritional information per serving: *Calories 332*

Total Fat 13.7g Saturated Fat 6.9g Cholesterol 102mg Sodium 350mg Carbohydrate 22.6g Dietary Fiber 2g Sugars 6g Protein 7.4g Calcium 143mg Phosphorous 186mg Potassium 74mg

Apple Cinnamon Rings

Cooking time: *20 minutes*

Servings: 6

Ingredients:

4 large apples, cut in rings

1 cup flour

¼ teaspoon baking powder

1 teaspoon stevia

¼ teaspoon cinnamon

1 large egg, beaten

1 cup milk

Vegetable oil, for frying

Cinnamon Topping:

⅓ cup of brown Swerve

2 teaspoons cinnamon

Direction:

Begin by mixing the flour with the baking powder, cinnamon, and stevia in a bowl.

Whisk the egg with the milk in a bowl.

Stir in the dry flour mixture and mix well until it makes a smooth batter.

Pour oil into a wok to deep fry the rings and heat it up to 375 degrees F.

First, dip the apple in the flour batter and deep fry until golden brown.

Transfer the apple rings on a tray lined with paper towel.

Drizzle the cinnamon and Swerve topping over the slices.

Serve fresh in the morning.

Nutritional information per serving: *Calories 166*

Total Fat 1.7g Saturated Fat 0.5g Cholesterol 33mg Sodium 55mg Carbohydrate 13.1g Dietary Fiber 1.9g Sugars 6.9g Protein 4.7g Calcium 65mg Phosphorous 241mg Potassium 197mg

Zucchini Bread

Cooking time: *1-hour* Servings: *16*

Ingredients:

3 eggs

1 1/2 cups Swerve

1 cup apple sauce

2 cups zucchini, shredded

1 teaspoon vanilla

2 cups flour

1/4 teaspoon baking powder

1 teaspoon baking soda

1 teaspoon cinnamon

1/2 teaspoon ginger

1 cup unsalted nuts, chopped

Direction:

Thoroughly whisk the eggs with the zucchini, apple sauce, and the rest of the ingredients in a bowl.

Once mixed evenly, spread the mixture in a loaf pan.

Bake it for 1 hour at 375 degrees F in a preheated oven.

Slice and serve.

Nutritional information per serving: *Calories 200*

Total Fat 5.4g Saturated Fat 0.9g Cholesterol 31mg Sodium 94mg Carbohydrate 26.9g Dietary Fiber 1.6g Sugars 16.3g Protein 4.4g Calcium 20mg Phosphorous 212mg Potassium 137mg

Garlic Mayo Bread

Cooking time: *5 minutes*

Servings: 16

Ingredients:

3 tablespoons vegetable oil

4 cloves garlic, minced

2 teaspoons paprika

Dash cayenne pepper

1 teaspoon lemon juice

2 tablespoons Parmesan cheese, grated

3/4 cup mayonnaise

1 loaf (1 lb.) French bread, sliced

1 teaspoon Italian herbs

Direction:

Mix the garlic with the oil in a small bowl and leave it overnight.

Discard the garlic from the bowl and keep the garlic-infused oil.

Mix the garlic-oil with cayenne, paprika, lemon juice, mayonnaise, and Parmesan.

Place the bread slices in a baking tray lined with parchment paper.

Top these slices with the mayonnaise mixture and drizzle the Italian herbs on top.

Broil these slices for 5 minutes until golden brown.

Serve warm.

Nutritional information per serving: *Calories 217*

Total Fat 7.9g Saturated Fat 1.8g Cholesterol 5mg Sodium 423mg Carbohydrate 30.3g Dietary Fiber 1.3g Sugars 2g Protein 7g Calcium 56mg Phosphorous 347mg Potassium 72mg

Strawberry Topped Waffles

Cooking time: 20 minutes

Servings: 5

Ingredients:

1 cup flour

1/4 cup Swerve

1 ¾ teaspoons baking powder

1 egg, separated

¾ cup milk

½ cup butter, melted

½ teaspoon vanilla extract

Fresh strawberries, sliced

Direction:

Prepare and preheat your waffle pan following the Direction of the machine.

Begin by mixing the flour with Swerve and baking soda in a bowl.

Separate the egg yolks from the egg whites, keeping them in two separate bowls.

Add the milk and vanilla extract to the egg yolks.

Stir the melted butter and mix well until smooth.

Now beat the egg whites with an electric beater until foamy and fluffy.

Fold this fluffy composition in the egg yolk mixture.

Mix it gently until smooth, then add in the flour mixture.

Stir again to make a smooth mixture.

Pour a half cup of the waffle batter in a preheated pan and cook until the waffle is done.

Cook more waffles with the remaining batter.

Serve fresh with strawberries on top.

Nutritional information per serving: *Calories 342*

Total Fat 20.5g Saturated Fat 12.5g Cholesterol 88mg Sodium 156mg Carbohydrate 21g Dietary Fiber 0.7g Sugars 3.5g Protein 4.8g Calcium 107mg Phosphorous 126mg Potassium 233mg

Mixed Pepper Mushroom Omelet

Cooking time: *10 minutes*

Servings: *2*

Ingredients:

1/4 cup green onions, chopped

1/4 cup fresh mushrooms, sliced

1/4 cup green pepper, chopped

2 tablespoons butter, divided

5 eggs

1/4 teaspoon pepper

1/4 cup Cheddar cheese, shredded

1/4 cup Monterey Jack cheese, shredded

Direction:

Begin by sautéing all the vegetables with the butter in a pan until crispy.

Whisk the eggs and black pepper until foamy and fluffy.

Spread this egg mixture over the vegetables in the pan and cover with a lid.

Cook for about 2 minutes, then flip the omelet with a spatula.

Drizzle the cheese on top and cover the lid for 2 more minutes.

Slice and serve.

Nutritional information per serving: *Calories 378*

Total Fat 31.5g Saturated Fat 16.4g Cholesterol 467mg Sodium 402mg Carbohydrate 3.1g Dietary Fiber 0.7g Sugars 1.7g Protein 21.6g Calcium 280mg Phosphorous 412mg Potassium 262mg

Simple Zucchini BBQ

Serving: 1

Preparation Time: 10 minutes

Cooking Time: 1-hour Ingredients:

Olive oil as needed

3 zucchinis

½ teaspoon black pepper

½ teaspoon mustard

½ teaspoon cumin

1 teaspoon paprika

1 teaspoon garlic powder

1 tablespoon of sea salt

1-2 stevia

1 tablespoon chili powder

Direction:

Preheat your oven to 300°F

Take a small bowl and add cayenne, black pepper, salt, garlic, mustard, paprika, chili powder, and stevia

Mix well

Slice zucchini into 1/8-inch slices and spray them with olive oil

Sprinkle spice blend over zucchini and bake for 40 minutes

Remove and flip, spray with more olive oil and leftover spice

Bake for 20 minutes more

Serve!

Nutrition (Per Serving)

Calories: 163

Fat: 14g

Carbohydrates: 3g

Protein: 8g

Bacon and Chicken Garlic Wrap

Serving: 4

Preparation Time: 15 minutes

Cooking Time: 10 minutes

Ingredients:

1 chicken fillet, cut into small cubes

8-9 thin slices of bacon, cut to fit cubes

6 garlic cloves, minced

Direction:

Preheat your oven to 400 °F Line a baking tray with aluminum foil

Add minced garlic to a bowl and rub each chicken piece with it

Wrap a bacon piece around each garlic chicken bite

Secure with a toothpick

Transfer bites to the baking sheet, keeping a little bit of space between them

Bake for about 15-20 minutes until crispy

Serve and enjoy!

Nutrition (Per Serving)

Calories: 260

Fat: 19g

Carbohydrates: 5g

Protein: 22g

Angel Eggs

Serving: 2

Preparation Time: 30 minutes
Cooking Time: Nil Ingredients:

4 eggs, hardboiled and peeled

1 tablespoon vanilla bean sweetener, sugar-free

2 tablespoons Keto-Friendly mayonnaise

1/8 teaspoon cinnamon

Direction:

Halve the boiled eggs and scoop out the yolk

Place in a bowl

Add egg whites on a plate

Add sweetener, cinnamon, mayo to the egg yolks and mash them well. Transfer the yolk mix to white halves

Nutrition (Per Serving)

Calories: 184

Fat: 15g

Carbohydrates: 1g

Protein: 12g

Omelet

Ingredients

5 big of eggs

2 green onion, cleaved

1 tablespoon 2% of milk

1/4 teaspoon dried basil

1/4 teaspoon dried oregano

Dash garlic powder

Dash salt

Dash pepper

2 tablespoons of butter

1/4 cup disintegrated feta cheddar

2 cuts store ham, slashed

1 plum tomato, slashed

2 teaspoons balsamic vinaigrette

Directions:

1.	In a little bowl, whisk eggs, green onion, milk, and seasonings until mixed. In an enormous nonstick skillet, heat margarine over medium-high warmth. Pour in egg blend. The blend should set promptly at the edge.

2.   As eggs set, push cooked segments toward the middle, giving uncooked eggs a chance to stream underneath. At the point when eggs are thickened and no fluid egg stays, top one side with cheddar and ham.

3.   Fold omelet down the middle; cut into two segments. Slide onto plates; top with tomato. Shower with vinaigrette before serving.

Nutrition Facts 1/2 omelet: 289 calories, 20g fat (9g immersed fat), 410mg cholesterol, 749mg sodium, 5g starch (3g sugars, 1g fiber), 21g protein.

Chapter 11: Lunch Recipes for the People with Kidney Problems

Chicken Noodle Soup

Preparation Time: 15 minutes

Cooking Time: 25 minutes

Servings: 4

Ingredients:

1 cup low-sodium chicken broth

1 cup water

1/4 teaspoon poultry seasoning

1/4 teaspoon black pepper

1/4 cup carrot, chopped

1 cup chicken, cooked and shredded

2 ounces egg noodles

Direction:

Add broth and water in a slow cooker.

Set the pot to high.

Add poultry seasoning and pepper.

Add carrot, chicken and egg noodles to the pot.

Cook on high setting for 25 minutes.

Serve while warm.

Nutrition:

Calories 141

Protein 15 g

Carbohydrates 11 g

Fat 4 g

Cholesterol 49 mg

Sodium 191 mg

Potassium 135 mg

Phosphorus 104 mg

Calcium 16 mg

Fiber 0.7 g

Beef Stew with Apple Cider

Preparation Time: 15 minutes

Cooking Time: 10 hours

Servings: 8

Ingredients:

1/2 cup potatoes, cubed

2 lb. beef cubes

7 tablespoons all-purpose flour, divided

1/4 teaspoon thyme

Black pepper to taste

3 tablespoons oil

¼ cup carrot, sliced

1 cup onion, diced

1/2 cup celery, diced

1 cup apples, diced

2 cups apple cider

1/2 cups water

2 tablespoons apple cider vinegar

Direction:

Double boil the potatoes (to reduce the amount of potassium) in a pot of water.

In a shallow dish, mix the half of the flour, thyme and pepper.

Coat all sides of beef cubes with the mixture.

In a pan over medium heat, add the oil and cook the beef cubes until brown. Set aside.

Layer the ingredients in your slow cooker.

Put the carrots, potatoes, onions, celery, beef and apple.

In a bowl, mix the cider, vinegar and 1 cup water.

Add this to the slow cooker.

Cook on low setting for 10 hours.

Stir in the remaining flour to thicken the soup.

Nutrition:

Calories 365

Protein 33 g

Carbohydrates 20 g

Fat 17 g

Cholesterol 73 mg

Sodium 80 mg

Potassium 540 mg

Phosphorus 234 mg

Calcium 36 mg

Fiber 2.2 g

Chicken Chili

Preparation Time: 20 minutes

Cooking Time: 1 hour and 15 minutes

Servings: 8

Ingredients:

1 tablespoon oil

1 cup onion, chopped

4 garlic cloves, chopped

1 cup green pepper

1 cup celery, chopped

1 cup carrots, chopped

14 oz. low-sodium chicken broth

1 lb. chicken breast, cubed and cooked

1 cup low-sodium tomatoes, drained and iced

1 cup kidney beans, rinsed and drained

3/4 cup salsa

3 tablespoons chili powder

1 teaspoon ground oregano

4 cups white rice, cooked

Direction:

In a pot, pour oil and cook onion, garlic, green pepper, celery and carrots.

Add the broth.

Bring to a boil.

Add the rest of the ingredients except the rice.

Simmer for 1 hour. Serve with rice.

Nutrition:

Calories 355

Protein 24 g

Carbohydrates 38 g

Fat 12 g

Cholesterol 59 mg

Sodium 348 mg

Potassium 653 mg

Phosphorus 270 mg

Calcium 133 mg

Fiber 4.7 g

Lamb Stew

Preparation Time: 30 minutes

Cooking Time: 1 hour and 40 minutes

Servings: 6

Ingredients:

1 lb. boneless lamb shoulder, trimmed and cubes

Black pepper to taste

1/4 cup all-purpose flour

1 tablespoon olive oil

1 onion, chopped

3 garlic cloves, chopped

1/2 cup tomato sauce

2 cups low-sodium beef broth

1 teaspoon dried thyme

2 parsnips, sliced

2 carrots, sliced

1 cup frozen peas

Direction:

Season lamb with pepper.

Coat evenly with flour.

Pour oil in a pot over medium heat.

Cook the lamb and then set aside.

Add onion to the pot.

Cook for 2 minutes.

Add garlic and saute for 30 seconds.

Pour in the broth to deglaze the pot.

Add the tomato sauce and thyme.

Put the lamb back to the pot.

Bring to a boil and then simmer for 1 hour.

Add parsnips and carrots.

Cook for 30 minutes.

Add green peas and cook for 5 minutes.

Nutrition:

Calories 283

Protein 27 g

Carbohydrates 19 g

Fat 11 g

Cholesterol 80 mg

Sodium 325 mg

Potassium 527 mg

Phosphorus 300 mg

Calcium 56 mg

Fiber 3.4 g

Tofu Stir Fry

Preparation Time: 15 minutes

Cooking Time: 20 minutes

Servings: 4

Ingredients:

1 teaspoon sugar

1 tablespoon lime juice

1 tablespoon low sodium soy sauce

2 tablespoons cornstarch

2 egg whites, beaten

1/2 cup unseasoned bread crumbs

1 tablespoon vegetable oil

16 ounces tofu, cubed

1 clove garlic, minced

1 tablespoon sesame oil

1 red bell pepper, sliced into strips

1 cup broccoli florets

1 teaspoon herb seasoning blend

Dash black pepper

Sesame seeds

Steamed white rice

Direction:

Dissolve sugar in a mixture of lime juice and soy sauce. Set aside.

In the first bowl, put the cornstarch.

Add the egg whites in the second bowl.

Place the breadcrumbs in the third bowl.

Dip each tofu cubes in the first, second and third bowls.

Pour vegetable oil in a pan over medium heat.

Cook tofu cubes until golden.

Drain the tofu and set aside.

Remove oil from the pan and add sesame oil.

Add garlic, bell pepper and broccoli.

Cook until crisp tender.

Season with the seasoning blend and pepper.

Put the tofu back and toss to mix.

Pour soy sauce mixture on top and transfer to serving bowls.

Garnish with the sesame seeds and serve on top of white rice.

Nutrition:

Calories 400

Protein 19 g

Carbohydrates 45 g

Fat 16 g

Cholesterol 0 mg

Sodium 584 mg

Potassium 317 mg

Phosphorus 177 mg

Calcium 253 mg

Fiber 2.7 g

Broccoli Pancake

Preparation Time: 10 minutes

Cooking Time: 5 minutes

Servings: 4

Ingredients:

3 cups broccoli florets, diced

2 eggs, beaten

2 tablespoons all-purpose flour

1/2 cup onion, chopped

2 tablespoons olive oil

Direction:

Boil broccoli in water for 5 minutes. Drain and set aside.

Mix egg and flour.

Add onion and broccoli to the mixture.

Pour oil in a pan over medium heat.

Cook the broccoli pancake until brown on both sides.

Nutrition:

Calories 140

Protein 6 g

Carbohydrates 7 g

Fat 10 g

Cholesterol 106 mg

Sodium 58 mg

Potassium 276 mg

Phosphorus 101 mg

Calcium 50 mg

Fiber 2.1 g

Carrot Casserole

Preparation Time: 10 minutes

Cooking Time: 20 minutes Serving: 8

Ingredients:

1 lb. carrots, sliced into rounds

12 low-sodium crackers

2 tablespoons butter

2 tablespoons onion, chopped

1/4 cup cheddar cheese, shredded

Direction:

Preheat your oven to 350 degrees F.

Boil carrots in a pot of water until tender.

Drain the carrots and reserve ¼ cup liquid.

Mash carrots.

Add all the ingredients into the carrots except cheese.

Place the mashed carrots in a casserole dish.

Sprinkle cheese on top and bake in the oven for 15 minutes.

Nutrition:

Calories 94

Protein 2 g

Carbohydrates 9 g

Fat 6 g

Cholesterol 13 mg

Sodium 174 mg

Potassium 153 mg

Phosphorus 47 mg

Calcium 66 mg

Fiber 1.8 g

Cauliflower Rice

Preparation Time: 10 minutes

Cooking Time: 10 minutes

Servings: 4

Ingredients:

1 head cauliflower, sliced into florets

1 tablespoon butter

Black pepper to taste

1/4 teaspoon garlic powder

1/4 teaspoon herb seasoning blend

Direction:

Put cauliflower florets in a food processor.

Pulse until consistency is similar to grain.

In a pan over medium heat, melt the butter and add the spices.

Toss cauliflower rice and cook for 10 minutes.

Fluff using a fork before serving.

Nutrition:

Calories 47

Protein 1 g

Carbohydrates 4 g

Fat 3 g

Cholesterol 8 mg

Sodium 43 mg

Potassium 206 mg

Phosphorus 31 mg

Calcium 16 mg

Fiber 1.4 g

Chicken Pineapple Curry

Cooking time: 3 hours 10 minutes

Servings: 6

Ingredients:

1 1/2 lbs. chicken thighs, boneless, skinless

1/2 teaspoon black pepper

1/2 teaspoon garlic powder

2 tablespoons olive oil

20 oz. canned pineapple

2 tablespoons brown Swerve

2 tablespoons soy sauce

1/2 teaspoon Tabasco sauce

2 tablespoons cornstarch

3 tablespoons water

Direction:

Begin by seasoning the chicken thighs with garlic powder and black pepper.

Set a suitable skillet over medium-high heat and add the oil to heat.

Add the boneless chicken to the skillet and cook for 3 minutes per side.

Transfer this seared chicken to a Slow cooker, greased with cooking spray.

Add 1 cup of the pineapple juice, Swerve, 1 cup of pineapple, tabasco sauce, and soy sauce to a slow cooker.

Cover the chicken-pineapple mixture and cook for 3 hours on low heat.

Transfer the chicken to the serving plates.

Mix the cornstarch with water in a small bowl and pour it into the pineapple curry.

Stir and cook this sauce for 2 minutes on high heat until it thickens.

Pour this sauce over the chicken and garnish with green onions.

Serve warm.

Nutritional information per serving: *Calories 256*

Total Fat 10.4g Saturated Fat 2.2g Cholesterol 67mg Sodium 371mg Total Carbohydrate 13.6g Dietary Fiber 1.5g Sugars 8.4g Protein 22.8g Calcium 28mg Phosphorous 107 mg Potassium 308mg

Baked Pork Chops

Cooking time: *40 minutes*

Servings: 6

Ingredients:

1/2 cup flour

1 large egg

1/4 cup water

3/4 cup breadcrumbs

6 (3 1/2 oz.) pork chops

2 tablespoons butter, unsalted

1 teaspoon paprika

Direction:

Begin by switching the oven to 350 degrees F to preheat.

Mix and spread the flour in a shallow plate.

Whisk the egg with water in another shallow bowl.

Spread the breadcrumbs on a separate plate.

Firstly, coat the pork with flour, then dip in the egg mix and then in the crumbs.

Grease a baking sheet and place the chops in it.

Drizzle the pepper on top and bake for 40 minutes.

Serve.

Nutritional information per serving: *Calories 221*

Total Fat 7.8g Saturated Fat 1.9g Cholesterol 93mg Sodium 135mg Carbohydrate 11.9g Dietary Fiber 3.5g Sugars 0.5g Protein 24.7g Calcium 13mg Phosphorous 299mg Potassium 391mg.

Lasagna Rolls in Marinara Sauce

Servings: 9

Cooking Time: 30 minutes

Ingredients:

¼ tsp crushed red pepper

¼ tsp salt

½ cup shredded mozzarella cheese

½ cups parmesan cheese, shredded

1 14-oz package tofu, cubed

1 25-oz can of low-sodium marinara sauce

1 tbsp extra virgin olive oil

12 whole wheat lasagna noodles

2 tbsp Kalamata olives, chopped

3 cloves minced garlic

3 cups spinach, chopped

Directions:

Put enough water on a large pot and cook the lasagna noodles according to package Direction. Drain, rinse and set aside until ready to use.

In a large skillet, sauté garlic over medium heat for 20 seconds. Add the tofu and spinach and cook until the spinach wilts. Transfer this mixture in a bowl and add parmesan olives, salt, red pepper and 2/3 cup of the marinara sauce.

In a pan, spread a cup of marinara sauce on the bottom. To make the rolls, place noodle on a surface and spread ¼ cup of the tofu filling. Roll up and place it on the pan with the marinara sauce. Do this procedure until all lasagna noodles are rolled.

Place the pan over high heat and bring to a simmer. Reduce the heat to medium and let it cook for three more minutes. Sprinkle mozzarella cheese and let the cheese melt for two minutes. Serve hot.

Nutrition Values:

Calories: 600; carbs: 65g; protein: 36g; fats: 26g; phosphorus: 627mg; potassium: 914mg; sodium: 1194mg.

Chicken Curry

Preparation Time: 10 Minutes

Cooking Time: 9 Hours

Servings: 5

Ingredients

2 to 3 boneless chicken breasts

¼ Cup of chopped green onions

1 can of 4 oz of diced green chilli peppers

2 Teaspoons of minced garlic

1 and 1/2 teaspoons of curry powder

1 Teaspoon of chili Powder

1 Teaspoon of cumin

½ Teaspoon of cinnamon

1 Teaspoon of lime juice

1 and 1/2 cups water

1 can or 7 oz of coconut milk

2 Cups of white cooked rice

Chopped cilantro, for garnish

Direction:

Combine the green onion with the chicken, the green chilli peppers, the garlic, the curry powder, the chilli powder, the cumin, the cinnamon, the lime juice, and the water in the bottom of a 6-qt slow cooker

Cover the slow cooker with a lid and cook your ingredients on Low for about 7 to 9 hours

After the cooking time ends up; shred the chicken with the help of a fork

Add in the coconut milk and cook on High for about 15 minutes

Top the chicken with cilantro; then serve your dish with rice

Enjoy your lunch!

Nutrition Information

Calories: 254, Fats: 18g, Carbs: 6g, Fiber: 1.6g, Potassium: 370mg, Sodium: 240mg, Phosphorous: 114mg, Protein 17g

Steak with Onion

Preparation Time: 5 Minutes

Cooking Time: 60 Minutes

Servings: 7-8

Ingredients:

¼ Cup of white flour

1/8 Teaspoon of ground black pepper

1 and ½ pounds of round steak of ¾ inch of thickness each

2 Tablespoons of oil

1 Cup of water

1 tablespoon of vinegar

1 Minced garlic clove

1 to 2 bay leaves

¼ teaspoon of crushed dried thyme

3 Sliced medium onions

Directions:

Cut the steak into about 7 to 8 equal servings. Combine the flour and the pepper; then pound the ingredients all together into the meat.

Heat the oil in a large skillet over a medium high heat and brown the meat on both its sides

Remove the meat from the skillet and set it aside

Combine the water with the vinegar, the garlic, the bay leaf and the thyme in the skillet; then bring the mixture to a boil

Place the meat in the mixture and cover it with onion slices

Cover your ingredients and let simmer for about 55 to 60 minutes

Serve and enjoy your lunch!

Nutrition Information

Calories: 286, Fats: 18g, Carbs: 12g, Fiber: 2.25g, Potassium: 368mg, Sodium: 45mg, Phosphorous: 180mg, Protein 19g

Shrimp Scampi

Preparation Time: 4 Minutes

Cooking Time: 8 Minutes

Servings: 3

Ingredients:

1 Tablespoon of olive oil

1 Minced garlic clove

½ Pound of cleaned and peeled shrimp

¼ Cup of dry white wine

1 Tablespoon of lemon juice

½ teaspoon of basil

1 tablespoon of chopped fresh parsley

4 Oz of dry linguini

Directions:

Heat the oil in a large non-stick skillet; then add the garlic and the shrimp and cook while stirring for about 4 minutes

Add the wine, the lemon juice, the basil and the parsley

Cook for about 5 minutes longer; then boil the linguini in unsalted water for a few minutes

Drain the linguini; then top it with the shrimp

Serve and enjoy your lunch!

Nutrition Information

Calories: 340, Fats: 26g, Carbs: 11.3g, Fiber: 2.1g, Potassium: 189mg, Sodium: 85mg, Phosphorous: 167mg, Protein 15g

Chicken Paella

Preparation Time: 5 Minutes

Cooking Time: 10 Minutes

Servings: 8

Ingredients:

½ Pound of skinned, boned and cut into pieces, chicken breasts

1/4 Cup of water

1 Can of 10-1/2 oz of low-sodium chicken broth

½ Pound of peeled and cleaned medium-size shrimp

1/2 Cup of frozen green pepper

1/3 cup of chopped red bell

1/3 cup of thinly sliced green onion

2 Minced garlic cloves

1/4 Teaspoon of pepper

1 Dash of ground saffron

1 Cup of uncooked instant white rice

Direction:

Combine the first 3 ingredients in medium casserole and cover it with a lid; then microwave it for about 4 minutes

Stir in the shrimp and the following 6 ingredients; then cover and microwave the shrimp on a high heat for about 3 and ½ minutes

Stir in the rice; then cover and set aside for about 5 minutes

Serve and enjoy your paella!

Nutrition Information

Calories: 236, Fats: 11g, Carbs: 6g, Fiber: 1.2g, Potassium: 178mg, Sodium: 83mg, Phosphorous: 144mg, Protein 28g

Beef Kabobs with Pepper

Preparation Time: 5 Minutes

Cooking Time: 10 Minutes

Servings: 8

Ingredients:

1 Pound of beef sirloin

½ Cup of vinegar

2 tbsp of salad oil

1 Medium, chopped onion

2 tbsp of chopped fresh parsley

¼ tsp of black pepper

2 Cut into strips green peppers

Directions:

Trim the fat from the meat; then cut it into cubes of 1 and ½ inches each

Mix the vinegar, the oil, the onion, the parsley and the pepper in a bowl

Place the meat in the marinade and set it aside for about 2 hours; make sure to stir from time to time.

Remove the meat from the marinade and alternate it on skewers instead with green pepper

Brush the pepper with the marinade and broil for about 10 minutes 4 inches from the heat

Serve and enjoy your kabobs

Nutrition Information

Calories: 357, Fats: 24g, Carbs: 9g, Fiber: 2.3g, Potassium: 250mg, Sodium: 60mg, Phosphorous: 217mg, Protein 26g

Chicken, Corn and Peppers

Preparation time: 5 minutes

Cooking Time: 1-hour Servings: 4

Ingredients:

2 pounds chicken breast, skinless, boneless and cubed

2 tablespoons olive oil

2 garlic cloves, minced

1 red onion, chopped

2 red bell peppers, chopped

¼ teaspoon cumin, ground

2 cups corn

½ cup chicken stock

1 teaspoon chili powder

¼ cup cilantro, chopped

Directions:

Heat up a pot with the oil over medium-high heat, add the chicken and brown for 4 minutes on each side.

Add the onion and the garlic and sauté for 5 minutes more.

Add the rest of the ingredients, stir, bring to a simmer over medium heat and cook for 45 minutes.

Divide into bowls and serve.

Nutrition: calories 332, fat 16.1, fiber 8.4, carbs 25.4, protein 17.4

Chapter 12: Dinner Recipes for the People with Kidney Problems

Lemon Pepper Trout

Cooking time: *15 minutes*

Servings: *2*

Ingredients:

1 lb. trout fillets

1 lb. asparagus

3 tablespoons olive oil

5 garlic cloves, minced

1/2 teaspoon black pepper

1/2 lemon, sliced

Direction:

Prepare and preheat the gas oven at 350 degrees F.

Rub the washed and dried fillets with oil then place them in a baking tray.

Top the fish with lemon slices, black pepper, and garlic cloves.

Spread the asparagus around the fish.

Bake the fish for 15 minutes approximately in the preheated oven.

Serve warm.

Nutritional information per serving: *Calories 336*

Total Fat 20.3g Saturated Fat 3.2g Cholesterol 84mg Sodium 370mg Carbohydrate 6.5g Dietary Fiber 2.7g Sugars 2.4g Protein 33g Calcium 100mg Phosphorous 107mg Potassium 383mg

Salmon Stuffed Pasta

Cooking time: *35 minutes*

Servings: *24*

Ingredients:

24 jumbo pasta shells, boiled

1 cup coffee creamer

Filling:

2 eggs, beaten

2 cups creamed cottage cheese

¼ cup chopped onion

1 red bell pepper, diced

2 teaspoons dried parsley

½ teaspoon lemon peel

1 can salmon, drained

Dill Sauce:

1 ½ teaspoon butter

1 ½ teaspoon flour

1/8 teaspoon pepper

1 tablespoon lemon juice

1 ½ cup coffee creamer

2 teaspoons dried dill weed

Direction:

Beat the egg with the cream cheese and all the other filling ingredients in a bowl.

Divide the filling in the pasta shells and place the shells in a 9x13 baking dish.

Pour the coffee creamer around the stuffed shells then cover with a foil.

Bake the shells for 30 minutes at 350 degrees F.

Meanwhile, whisk all the ingredients for dill sauce in a saucepan.

Stir for 5 minutes until it thickens.

Pour this sauce over the baked pasta shells.

Serve warm.

Nutritional information per serving: *Calories 268*

Total Fat 4.8g Saturated Fat 2g Cholesterol 27mg Sodium 86mg Total Carbohydrate 42.6g Dietary Fiber 2.1g Sugars

2.4g Protein 11.5g Calcium 27mg Phosphorous 314mg Potassium 181mg

Tuna Casserole

Preparation Time: 15 minutes

Cooking time: 35 minutes

Servings:4

Ingredients:

½ cup Cheddar cheese, shredded

2 tomatoes, chopped

7 oz tuna filet, chopped

1 teaspoon ground coriander

½ teaspoon salt

1 teaspoon olive oil

½ teaspoon dried oregano

Directions:

Brush the casserole mold with olive oil.

Mix up together chopped tuna fillet with dried oregano and ground coriander.

Place the fish in the mold and flatten well to get the layer.

Then add chopped tomatoes and shredded cheese.

Cover the casserole with foil and secure the edges.

Bake the meal for 35 minutes at 355F.

Nutrition: calories 260, fat 21.5, fiber 0.8, carbs 2.7, protein 14.6

Oregano Salmon with Crunchy Crust

Preparation Time: 10 minutes

Cooking time: 2 hours

Servings:2

Ingredients:

8 oz salmon fillet

2 tablespoons panko bread crumbs

1 oz Parmesan, grated

1 teaspoon dried oregano

1 teaspoon sunflower oil

Directions:

In the mixing bowl combine together panko bread crumbs, Parmesan, and dried oregano.

Sprinkle the salmon with olive oil and coat in the breadcrumb's mixture.

After this, line the baking tray with baking paper.

Place the salmon in the tray and transfer in the preheated to the 385F oven.

Bake the salmon for 25 minutes.

Nutrition: calories 245, fat 12.8, fiber 0.6, carbs 5.9, protein 27.5

Sardine Fish Cakes

Preparation Time: 10 minutes

Cooking time: 10 minutes

Servings:4

Ingredients:

11 oz sardines, canned, drained

1/3 cup shallot, chopped

1 teaspoon chili flakes

½ teaspoon salt

2 tablespoon wheat flour, whole grain

1 egg, beaten

1 tablespoon chives, chopped

1 teaspoon olive oil

1 teaspoon butter

Directions:

Put the butter in the skillet and melt it.

Add shallot and cook it until translucent.

After this, transfer the shallot in the mixing bowl.

Add sardines, chili flakes, salt, flour, egg, chives, and mix up until smooth with the help of the fork.

Make the medium size cakes and place them in the skillet.

Add olive oil.

Roast the fish cakes for 3 minutes from each side over the medium heat.

Dry the cooked fish cakes with the paper towel if needed and transfer in the serving plates.

Nutrition: calories 221, fat 12.2, fiber 0.1, carbs 5.4, protein 21.3

Cajun Catfish

Preparation Time: 10 minutes

Cooking time: 10 minutes

Servings:4

Ingredients:

16 oz catfish steaks (4 oz each fish steak)

1 tablespoon cajun spices

1 egg, beaten

1 tablespoon sunflower oil

Directions:

Pour sunflower oil in the skillet and preheat it until shimmering.

Meanwhile, dip every catfish steak in the beaten egg and coat in Cajun spices.

Place the fish steaks in the hot oil and roast them for 4 minutes from each side.

The cooked catfish steaks should have a light brown crust.

Nutrition: calories 263, fat 16.7, fiber 0, carbs 0.1, protein 26.3

Teriyaki Tuna

Preparation Time: 10 minutes

Cooking time: 6 minutes

Servings:3

Ingredients:

3 tuna fillets

3 teaspoons teriyaki sauce

½ teaspoon minced garlic

1 teaspoon olive oil

Directions:

Whisk together teriyaki sauce, minced garlic, and olive oil.

Brush every tuna fillet with teriyaki mixture.

Preheat grill to 390F.

Grill the fish for 3 minutes from each side.

Nutrition: calories 382, fat 32.6, fiber 0, carbs 1.1, protein 21.4

Herbed Vegetable Trout

Cooking time: 15 minutes

Servings: 4

Ingredients:

14 oz. trout fillets

1/2 teaspoon herb seasoning blend

1 lemon, sliced

2 green onions, sliced

1 stalk celery, chopped

1 medium carrot, julienne

Direction:

Prepare and preheat a charcoal grill over moderate heat.

Place the trout fillets over a large piece of foil and drizzle herb seasoning on top.

Spread the lemon slices, carrots, celery, and green onions over the fish.

Cover the fish with foil and pack it.

Place the packed fish in the grill and cook for 15 minutes.

Once done, remove the foil from the fish.

Serve.

Nutritional information per serving: *Calories 202*

Total Fat 8.5g Saturated Fat 1.5g Cholesterol 73mg Sodium 82mg Carbohydrate 3.5g Dietary Fiber 1.1g Sugars 1.3g Protein 26.9g Calcium 70mg Phosphorous 287mg Potassium 560mg

Citrus Glazed Salmon

Cooking time: *17 minutes*

Servings: *4*

Ingredients:

2 garlic cloves, crushed

1 1/2 tablespoons lemon juice

2 tablespoons olive oil

1 tablespoon butter

1 tablespoon Dijon mustard

2 dashes cayenne pepper

1 teaspoon dried basil leaves

1 teaspoon dried dill

24 oz. salmon filet

Direction:

Place a 1-quart saucepan over moderate heat and add the oil, butter, garlic, lemon juice, mustard, cayenne pepper, dill, and basil to the pan.

Stir this mixture for 5 minutes after it has boiled.

Prepare and preheat a charcoal grill over moderate heat.

Place the fish on a foil sheet and fold the edges to make a foil tray.

Pour the prepared sauce over the fish.

Place the fish in the foil in the preheated grill and cook for 12 minutes.

Slice and serve.

Nutritional information per serving: *Calories 401*

Total Fat 20.5g Saturated Fat 5.3g Cholesterol 144mg Sodium 256mg Carbohydrate 0.5g Dietary Fiber 0.2g Sugars 0.1g Protein 48.4g Calcium 549mg Phosphorous 214mg Potassium 446mg

Broiled Salmon Fillets

Cooking time: 13 minutes

Servings*:* 4

Ingredients:

1 tablespoon ginger root, grated

1 clove garlic, minced

¼ cup maple syrup

1 tablespoon hot pepper sauce

4 salmon fillets, skinless

Direction:

Grease a pan with cooking spray and place it over moderate heat.

Add the ginger and garlic and sauté for 3 minutes then transfer to a bowl.

Add the hot pepper sauce and maple syrup to the ginger-garlic.

Mix well and keep this mixture aside.

Place the salmon fillet in a suitable baking tray, greased with cooking oil.

Brush the maple sauce over the fillets liberally

Broil them for 10 minutes at the oven at broiler settings.

Serve warm.

Nutritional information per serving: *Calories 289*

Total Fat 11.1g Saturated Fat 1.6g Cholesterol 78mg Sodium 80mg Carbohydrate 13.6g Dietary Fiber 0g Sugars 11.8g Protein 34.6g Calcium 78mg Phosphorous 230mg Potassium 331mg

Crab Cakes

Cooking time: *20 minutes*

Servings: *4*

Ingredients:

1 lb. crab meat

1 egg

1/3 cup bell pepper, chopped

1/4 cup onion, chopped

¼ cup panko breadcrumbs

1/4 cup mayonnaise

1 tablespoon dry mustard

1 teaspoon black pepper

2 tablespoons lemon juice

1 tablespoon garlic powder

dash cayenne pepper

3 tablespoons olive oil

Direction:

Mix the crab meat with all the spices, veggies, crackers, egg, and mayonnaise in a suitable bowl.

Once it is well mixed, make 4 patties out of this mixture.

Grease a suitable skillet and place it over moderate heat.

Sear each Pattie for 5 minutes per side in the hot pan.

Serve.

Nutritional information per serving: *Calories 315*

Total Fat 20.4g Saturated Fat 2.9g Cholesterol 105mg Sodium 844mg Carbohydrate 13g Dietary Fiber 1.3g Sugars 3.3g Protein 17.4g Calcium 437mg Phosphorous 288mg Potassium 114mg

Broiled Shrimp

Cooking time: *5 minutes*

Servings: 8

Ingredients:

1 lb. shrimp in shell

1/2 cup unsalted butter, melted

2 teaspoons lemon juice

2 tablespoons chopped onion

1 clove garlic, minced

1/8 teaspoon pepper

Direction:

Toss the shrimp with the butter, lemon juice, onion, garlic, and pepper in a bowl. Spread the seasoned shrimp in a baking tray. Broil for 5 minutes in an oven on broiler setting.

Serve warm. Nutritional information per serving: *Calories 164*

Total Fat 12.8g, Saturated Fat 7.4g, Cholesterol 167mg, Sodium 242mg, Carbohydrate 0.6g, Dietary Fiber 0.1g, Sugars 0.2g, Protein 14.6g, Calcium 45mg, Phosphorous 215mg, Potassium 228mg.

Grilled Lemony Cod

Cooking time: *10 minutes*

Servings: *4*

Ingredients:

1 lb. cod fillets

1 teaspoon salt-free lemon pepper seasoning

1/4 cup lemon juice

Direction:

Rub the cod fillets with lemon pepper seasoning and lemon juice.

Grease a baking tray with cooking spray and place the salmon in the baking tray.

Bake the fish for 10 minutes at 350 degrees F in a preheated oven.

Serve warm.

Nutritional information per serving: *Calories 155*

Total Fat 7.1g Saturated Fat 1.1g Cholesterol 50mg Sodium 53mg Carbohydrate 0.7g Dietary Fiber 0.2g Sugars 0.3g Protein 22.2g Calcium 43mg Phosphorous 237mg Potassium 461mg

Chapter 13: Juice and Smoothies Recipes for the People with Kidney Problems

Winter Berry Smoothie

Servings: 2

Preparation time: 5 minutes Vibrant in color and vitamins alike.

Ingredients:

1/4 cup blackberries

1/4 cup cherries, pitted

1/4 cup cranberries

2 cups water

Direction

Blend until smooth in a blender or smoothie maker.

Serve right away.

Per Serving: Calories 21

Protein 2 g Carbohydrates 5 g Fat 0 g

Sodium 1 mg Potassium 62 mg Phosphorus 10 mg

Carrot Smoothie

Ingredients

1 cup cut carrots

½ teaspoon finely destroyed orange strip

1 cup squeezed orange

1½ cups ice 3D shapes

Orange strip twists (discretionary)

Directions:

1.   In a secured little pan, cook carrots in a modest quantity of bubbling water around 15 minutes or until delicate. Channel well. Cool.

2.   Spot depleted carrots in a blender. Include finely destroyed orange strip and squeezed orange. Cover and mix until smooth. Include ice blocks; cover and mix until smooth. Fill glasses. Whenever wanted, decorate with orange strip twists.

Strawberry Papaya Smoothie

Ingredients:

½ cup of strawberries

2 cups of sliced papaya

2 cup of coconut kefir

2 scoop of vanilla bone broth protein powder

½ cup of ice water

Directions:

Did you realize that papaya is incredible for digestion? The tropical organic product is stacked with compounds and cell reinforcements that help the body detox and decrease irritation. It's likewise a too delectable element for smoothies. In case you're hoping to switch up your typical formula, it's a great opportunity to attempt this Strawberry Papaya Smoothie. You will need to add all the above ingredients to blender & blend on high.

This beverage is without dairy and utilizations coconut kefir for the help of a probiotic. At the point when blended in with vanilla protein powder and crisp strawberries, you have a simple, in a hurried breakfast or post-exercise supper to fuel your body.

Add every one of the ingredients to the blender, and mix until the Strawberry Papaya Smoothie is pleasantly joined. I love including a crisp sprig of mint to supplement this new and fruity smoothie.

Gut Cleansing Smoothie

Serving: 1

Preparation Time: 10 minutes

Ingredients:

1 ½ tablespoons coconut oil, unrefined

½ cup plain full-fat yogurt

1 tablespoon chia seeds

1 serving aloe vera leaves

½ cup frozen blueberries, unsweetened

1 tablespoon hemp hearts

1 cup of water

1 scoop Pinnaclife prebiotic fiber

Directions:

Add listed ingredients to a blender

Blend until you have a smooth and creamy texture

Serve chilled and enjoy!

Nutrition (Per Serving)

Calories: 409

Fat: 33g

Carbohydrates: 8g

Protein: 12g

Cabbage and Chia Glass

Serving: 2

Preparation Time: 10 minutes

Ingredients:

1/3 cup cabbage

1 cup cold unsweetened almond milk

1 tablespoon chia seeds

½ cup cherries

½ cup lettuce

Directions:

Add coconut milk to your blender

Cut cabbage and add to your blender

Place chia seeds in a coffee grinder and chop to powder, brush the powder into a blender

Pit the cherries and add them to the blender

Wash and dry the lettuce and chop

Add to the mix

Cover and blend on low followed by medium

Taste the texture and serve chilled!

Nutrition (Per Serving)

Calories: 409

Fat: 33g

Carbohydrates: 8g

Protein: 12g

Blueberry and Kale Mix

Serving: 1

Preparation Time: 10 minutes

Ingredients:

½ cup low-fat Greek Yogurt

1 cup baby kale greens

1 pack stevia

1 tablespoon MCT oil

¼ cup blueberries

1 tablespoon pepitas

1 tablespoon flaxseed, ground

1 ½ cups of water

Directions:

Add listed ingredients to a blender

Blend until you have a smooth and creamy texture

Serve chilled and enjoy!

Nutrition (Per Serving)

Calories: 307

Fat: 24g

Carbohydrates: 14g

Protein: 9g

Blackberry-Sage Drink

Preparation time: *10 minutes*

Servings: *8*

Ingredients

1 cup fresh blackberries

4 sage leaves

10 cups water

Direction

Add blackberries, sage leave, and 10 cup water to a blender.

Blend well, then strain and refrigerate to chill.

Serve.

Nutritional Values

Calories: 7

Protein: 0 g

Carbohydrates: 2 g

Fat: 0 g

Cholesterol: 0 mg

Sodium: 7 mg

Potassium: 26 mg

Phosphorus: 3 mg

Calcium: 13 mg

Fiber: 0.7 g

Beet Juice Blend

Preparation time: *10 minutes*

Servings: *2*

Ingredients

½ medium apple

½ medium beet

1 medium fresh carrot

1 celery stalk

¼ cup parsley

Direction

Pass apple, beet, celery, parsley, and carrot through a juicer.

Divide this juice into two serving glasses, then refrigerate to chill.

Serve.

Nutritional Values

Calories: 186

Protein: 23 g

Carbohydrates: 19 g

Fat: 2 g

Cholesterol: 41 mg

Sodium: 62 mg

Potassium: 282 mg

Phosphorus: 118 mg

Calcium: 160 mg

Fiber: 1.1 g

Pineapple Smoothie

Preparation time: 10 minutes

Servings: 1

Ingredients:

1 cup coconut water

1 orange, peeled and cut into quarters

1½ cups pineapple chunks

1 tablespoon fresh grated ginger

1 teaspoon chia seeds

1 teaspoon turmeric powder

A pinch of black pepper

Directions:

In your blender, mix the coconut water with the orange, pineapple, ginger, chia seeds, turmeric and black pepper. Pulse well, pour into a glass and serve for breakfast.

Enjoy!

Nutrition: calories 151, fat 2, fiber 6, carbs 12, protein 4

Cucumber and Pineapple Smoothie

Preparation time: 10 minutes

Servings: 2

Ingredients:

2 cups kale, torn

1 cup brewed green tea

1 cup pineapple chunks

1 cup cucumber, peeled and chopped

½ cup mango chunks, frozen

½ banana, peeled

1 teaspoon ground ginger

¼ teaspoon ground turmeric

3 mint leaves, chopped

1 tablespoon chia seeds

4 ice cubes

1 scoop protein powder

Directions:

In your blender, mix the kale with the green tea, pineapple, cucumber, mango, banana, ginger, turmeric, mint, protein powder and ice. Pulse well then add the chia seeds. Stir, divide into 2 glasses and serve.

Enjoy!

Nutrition: calories 161, fat 2, fiber 6, carbs 11, protein 5

Cinnamon Smoothie

Preparation time: *10 minutes*

Servings: 2

Ingredients

½ teaspoon ground cinnamon

1 tablespoon sugar

1/8 teaspoon vanilla extract

8 ounces egg white

3 tablespoons whipped topping

Direction

Mix cinnamon, sugar, 2 ounces egg whites, and vanilla in a mixer.

Serve with whipped topping.

Enjoy.

Nutritional Values

Calories: 207

Protein: 28 g

Carbohydrates: 17 g

Fat: 3 g

Cholesterol: 0 mg

Sodium: 428 mg

Potassium: 427 mg

Phosphorus: 39 mg

Calcium: 30 mg

Fiber: 0.6 g

Cinnamon Egg Smoothie

Cooking time: *0 minutes*

Servings: *2*

Ingredients:

1/2 teaspoon ground cinnamon

1 teaspoon stevia

1/8 teaspoon vanilla extract

8 oz. egg white, pasteurized

3 tablespoons whipped topping

Direction:

Mix the stevia, egg whites, cinnamon, and vanilla in a mixer.

Serve with whipped topping.

Enjoy.

Nutritional information per serving: *Calories 95*

Total Fat 1.2g Saturated Fat 0.6g Cholesterol 3mg Sodium 120mg Carbohydrate 3.1g Dietary Fiber 0.3g Sugars 0.8g Protein 12.5g Calcium 18mg Phosphorous 185mg Potassium 194mg

Pineapple Sorbet Smoothie

Cooking time: 0 minutes

Servings: 1

Ingredients:

3/4 cup pineapple sorbet

1 scoop protein powder

1/2 cup water

2 ice cubes, optional

Direction:

First, begin by putting everything into a blender jug.

Pulse it for 30 seconds until well blended.

Serve chilled.

Nutritional information per serving: *Calories 180*

Total Fat 1g Saturated Fat 0.5g Cholesterol 40mg Sodium 86mg Carbohydrate 30.5g Dietary Fiber 0g Sugars 28g Protein 13g Calcium 9mg Phosphorous 164mg Potassium 111mg

Vanilla Fruit Smoothie

Cooking time: 0 minutes

Servings: 2

Ingredients:

2 oz. mango, peeled and cubed

2 oz. strawberries

2 oz. avocado flesh, cubed

2 oz. banana, peeled

2 scoops of protein powder

1 cup cold water

1 cup crushed ice

Direction:

First, begin by putting everything into a blender jug.

Pulse it for 30 seconds until well blended.

Serve chilled.

Nutritional information per serving: *Calories 228*

Total Fat 7.6g Saturated Fat 2.1g Cholesterol 65mg Sodium 58mg Total Carbohydrate 19g Dietary Fiber 3.6g Sugars 9.8g

Protein 23.4g Calcium 112mg Phosphorous 216 mg
Potassium 504mg

Protein Berry Smoothie

Cooking time: *0 minutes*

Servings: *2*

Ingredients:

4 oz. water

1 cup frozen mixed berries

2 ice cubes

1 teaspoon blueberry essence

2 scoops whey protein powder

Direction:

First, begin by putting everything into a blender jug.

Pulse it for 30 seconds until well blended.

Serve chilled.

Nutritional information per serving: *Calories 248*

Total Fat 11.4g Saturated Fat 6.7g Cholesterol 98mg Sodium 67mg Carbohydrate 13.3g Dietary Fiber 2.5g Sugars 6.1g Protein 23.3g Calcium 132mg Phosphorous 152mg Potassium 296mg

Protein Peach Smoothie

Cooking time: 0 minutes

Servings: 1

Ingredients:

1/2 cup ice

2 tablespoons egg whites, pasteurized

3/4 cup fresh peaches

1 teaspoon stevia

Direction:

First, begin by putting everything into a blender jug.

Pulse it for 30 seconds until well blended.

Serve chilled.

Nutritional information per serving: *Calories 195*

Total Fat 0.3g Saturated Fat 0g Cholesterol 0mg Sodium 347mg Carbohydrate 17g Dietary Fiber 1.7g Sugars 14.2g Protein 24.1g Calcium 25mg Phosphorous 233mg Potassium 526mg

Cranberry Cucumber Smoothie

Cooking time: *0 minutes*

Servings: *1*

Ingredients:

1 cup frozen cranberries

1 medium cucumber, peeled and sliced

1 stalk of celery

1 teaspoon lime juice

Direction:

First, begin by putting everything into a blender jug.

Pulse it for 30 seconds until well blended.

Serve chilled.

Nutritional information per serving: *Calories 119*

Total Fat 0.4g Saturated Fat 0.1g Cholesterol 0mg Sodium 21mg Carbohydrate 25.1g Dietary Fiber 6g Sugars 10g Protein 2.3g Calcium 79mg Phosphorous 184mg Potassium 325mg

Raspberry Smoothie

Cooking time: 0 minutes

Servings: 2

Ingredients:

1 cup frozen raspberries

1 medium peach, pitted, sliced

½ cup tofu

1 tablespoon honey

1 cup milk

Direction:

First, begin by putting everything into a blender jug.

Pulse it for 30 seconds until well blended.

Serve chilled.

Nutritional information per serving: *Calories 223*

Total Fat 2.7g Saturated Fat 0.3g Cholesterol 0mg Sodium 99mg Carbohydrate 49.9g Dietary Fiber 7.2g Sugars 43.1g Protein 3.6g Calcium 176mg Phosphorous 95mg Potassium 426mg

Citrus Pineapple Shake

Cooking time: 0 minutes

Servings: 2

Ingredients:

1/2 cup pineapple juice

1/2 cup almond milk

1 cup orange sherbet

1/2 cup egg, pasteurized

Direction:

Pour the almond milk, pineapple juice, sherbet, and egg into the blender.

Blend well for 1 minute then refrigerate to chill.

Serve.

Nutritional information per serving: *Calories 242*

Total Fat 8.2g Saturated Fat 2.8g Cholesterol 227mg Sodium 155mg Carbohydrate 33g Dietary Fiber 1.1g Sugars 26.2g Protein 8.9g Calcium 80mg Phosphorous 121mg Potassium 234mg

Pineapple Smoothie

Cooking time: 0 minutes

Servings: 2

Ingredients:

3/4 cup pineapple sherbet

1 scoop protein powder

1/2 cup water

2 ice cubes

Direction:

Add the water, pineapple sherbet, protein powder, and ice to a blender.

Blend the pineapple smoothie for 1 minute.

Serve.

Nutritional information per serving: *Calories 91*

Total Fat 0.6g Saturated Fat 0.2g Cholesterol 7mg Sodium 36mg Carbohydrate 10.4g Dietary Fiber 0g Sugars 8g Protein 11.9g Calcium 208mg Phosphorous 49mg Potassium 25mg

Chapter 14: Dessert Recipes for the People with Kidney Problems

Cream Cheese Tarts

Preparation time: *10 minutes*

Cooking Time: *10 minutes* Total time: *20 minutes*

Servings: 6

Ingredients

8 ounces cream cheese

2 eggs

¾ cup sugar

2 teaspoons vanilla extract

2 dozen paper cupcake liners

2 dozen vanilla wafers

1 ½ cups apple pie filling

Direction

Preheat oven to 350°F.

Beat cream cheese with sugar, vanilla extract, and eggs in a mixer until smooth.

Layer a muffin tray with muffin cups and place one vanilla wafer in each cup.

Divide the cream cheese mixture into the cups, then bake for 10 minutes.

Allow it to cool then refrigerate for 2 hours.

Serve.

Nutritional Values

Calories: 136

Protein: 2 g

Carbohydrates: 14 g

Fat: 8 g

Cholesterol: 28 mg

Sodium: 78 mg

Potassium: 49 mg

Phosphorus: 27 mg

Calcium: 18 mg

Fiber: 0.2 g

Orange Biscotti

Preparation time: *10 minutes*

Cooking Time: *25 minutes* Total time: *35 minutes*

Servings: *8*

Ingredients

2 ½ cups all-purpose flour

2 teaspoons baking powder

2 teaspoons anise seed

1 teaspoon orange rind, grated

½ cup sugar

1 large egg

2 tablespoons canola oil

1 teaspoon orange extract

Direction

Layer a cookie sheet with a parchment sheet and keep it aside.

Preheat oven to 350°F.

Whisk flour, baking powder, anise seed, orange rind, and sugar in a bowl.

Beat egg with orange extract and oil in a mixer until frothy.

Add this egg-orange mixture to the flour mixture and mix well to form a biscotti dough.

Make 12-inch long biscottis out of the dough and place them on the cookie sheet.

Bake these biscotti for 20 minutes in the preheated oven.

Flip all the biscotti and bake for another 5 minutes.

Serve.

Nutritional Values

Calories: 98

Protein: 2 g

Carbohydrates: 18 g

Fat: 2 g

Cholesterol: 12 mg

Sodium: 45 mg

Potassium: 26 mg

Phosphorus: 76 mg

Calcium: 43 mg

Fiber: 0.5 g

Strawberry Delight

Preparation time: *10 minutes*

Cooking Time: 45 minutes Total time: *55 minutes*

Servings: 6

Ingredients

1 package angel food cake mix

8 ounces whipped cream cheese

½ cup strawberry preserves

2 cups whipped topping

Direction

Bake the cake using the cake mix as per the package's Direction.

Meanwhile, beat cream cheese with strawberry preserves in a mixer until smooth.

Fold in whipped topping and mix gently.

Slice the baked cake into three layers, horizontally.

Spread 1/3 of the cream cheese filling over one cake layer.

Place the second layer on top of it and spread the 1/3 cream cheese filling over this cake.

Lastly, place the third cake slice over it and top it with remaining cream cheese filling.

Refrigerate the layered cake for 4 hours.

Slice and serve.

Nutritional Values

Calories: 278

Protein: 5 g

Carbohydrates: 42 g

Fat: 10 g

Cholesterol: 33 mg

Sodium: 367 mg

Potassium: 125 mg

Phosphorus: 155 mg

Calcium: 81 mg

Fiber: 0 g

Lemon Squares

Preparation time: *10 minutes*

Cooking Time: *35 minutes* Total time: *45 minutes*

Servings: *12*

Ingredients

1 cup powdered sugar

1 cup all-purpose white flour

½ cup unsalted butter

1 cup granulated sugar

½ teaspoon baking powder

2 eggs, slightly beaten

4 tablespoons lemon juice

1 tablespoon unsalted butter, softened

1 tablespoon lemon rind, grated

Direction

Start mixing ¼ cup confectioner's sugar, ½ cup butter, and flour in a bowl.

Spread this crust mixture in an 8-inch square pan and press it.

Bake this flour crust for 15 minutes at 350°F.

Meanwhile, prepare the filling by beating granulated sugar, 2 tablespoons lemon juice, lemon rind, eggs, and baking powder in a mixer.

Spread this filling in the baked crust and bake again for 20 minutes.

Prepare the icing meanwhile by beating 1 tablespoon butter with 2 tablespoons lemon juice and ¾ cup confectioners' sugar.

Once the lemon pie is baked, allow it to cool.

Drizzle the icing mixture on top of the lemon pie then cut it into 36 squares.

Serve.

Nutritional Values

Calories: 146

Protein: 2 g

Carbohydrates: 22 g

Fat: 6 g

Cholesterol: 39 mg

Sodium: 45 mg

Potassium: 22 mg

Phosphorus: 32 mg

Calcium: 16 mg

Fiber: 0.2 g

Creamy Pineapple Dessert

Preparation time: *10 minutes*

Cooking Time: *0 minutes* Total time: *10 minutes*

Servings: *2*

Ingredients

16 ounces cottage cheese

15 ounces canned pineapple

8 ounces whipped topping

½ teaspoon green food coloring

Direction

Throw all the dessert ingredients into a suitably-sized bowl.

Mix them well and refrigerate for 1 hour.

Serve.

Nutritional Values

Calories: 204

Protein: 10 g

Carbohydrates: 23 g

Fat: 8 g

Cholesterol: 13 mg

Sodium: 303 mg

Potassium: 203 mg

Phosphorus: 152 mg

Calcium: 100 mg

Fiber: 0.6 g

Blackberry Mountain Pie

Preparation time: *10 minutes*

Cooking Time: *45 minutes* Total time: *55 minutes*

Servings: *8*

Ingredients

1/3 cup unsalted butter

4 cups blackberries

13 tablespoons sugar

1 cup all-purpose white flour

½ teaspoon baking powder

¾ cup Rice Drink

Direction

Preheat oven to 375°F.

Grease a 2-quart baking dish with melted butter.

Toss blackberries with 1 tablespoon sugar in a small bowl.

Whisk the remaining ingredients in a mixer until they form a smooth batter.

Spread this pie batter in the prepared baking dish and top it with blackberries.

Bake the blackberry pie for 45 minutes in the preheated oven.

Slice and serve once chilled.

Nutritional Values

Calories: 320

Protein: 4 g

Carbohydrates: 49 g

Fat: 12 g

Cholesterol: 28 mg

Sodium: 222 mg

Potassium: 186 mg

Phosphorus: 91 mg

Calcium: 65 mg

Fiber: 5.6 g

Buttery Lemon Squares

Cooking time: *35 minutes*

Servings: *12*

Ingredients:

1 cup refined Swerve

1 cup flour

1/2 cup butter, unsalted

1 cup granulated Swerve

1/2 teaspoon baking powder

2 eggs, beaten

4 tablespoons lemon juice

1 tablespoon butter, unsalted, softened

1 tablespoon lemon zest

Direction:

Start mixing ¼ cup refined Swerve, ½ cup butter, and flour in a bowl.

Spread this crust mixture in an 8-inche square pan and press it.

Bake this flour crust for 15 minutes at 350 degrees F.

Meanwhile, prepare the filling by beating 2 tablespoons lemon juice, granulated Swerve, eggs, lemon rind, and baking powder in a mixer.

Spread this filling in the baked crust and bake again for about 20 minutes.

Meanwhile, prepare the squares' icing by beating 2 tablespoons lemon juice, 1 tablespoon butter, and ¾ cup refine Swerve.

Once the lemon pie is baked well, allow it to cool.

Sprinkle the icing mixture on top of the lemon pie then cut it into 36 squares.

Serve.

Nutritional information per serving: *Calories 229*

Total Fat 9.5g Saturated Fat 5.8g Cholesterol 50mg Sodium 66mg Carbohydrate 22.8g Dietary Fiber 0.3g Sugars 16g Protein 2.1g Calcium 18mg Phosphorous 257mg Potassium 51mg

Chocolate Gelatin Mousse

Cooking time: 5 minutes

Servings: 4

Ingredients:

1 teaspoon stevia

1/2 teaspoon gelatin

1/4 cup milk

1/2 cup chocolate chips

1 teaspoon vanilla

1/2 cup heavy cream, whipped

Direction:

Whisk the stevia with the gelatin and milk in a saucepan and cook up to a boil.

Stir in the chocolate and vanilla then mix well until it has completely melted.

Beat the cream in a mixer until fluffy then fold in the chocolate mixture.

Mix it gently with a spatula then transfer to the serving bowl.

Refrigerate the dessert for 4 hours.

Serve.

Nutritional information per serving: *Calories 200*

Total Fat 12.1g Saturated Fat 8g Cholesterol 27mg Sodium 31mg Carbohydrate 4.7g Dietary Fiber 0.7g Sugars 0.8g Protein 3.2g Calcium 68mg Phosphorous 120mg Potassium 100mg

Blackberry Cream Cheese Pie

Cooking time: *45 minutes*
Servings: *8*

Ingredients:

1/3 cup butter, unsalted

4 cups blackberries

1 teaspoon stevia

1 cup flour

1/2 teaspoon baking powder

3/4 cup cream cheese

Direction:

Switch your gas oven to 375 degrees F to preheat.

Layer a 2-quart baking dish with melted butter.

Mix the blackberries with stevia in a small bowl.

Beat the remaining ingredients in a mixer until they form a smooth batter.

Evenly spread this pie batter in the prepared baking dish and top it with blackberries.

Bake the blackberry pie for about 45 minutes in the preheated oven.

Slice and serve once chilled.

Nutritional information per serving: *Calories 239*

Total Fat 8.4g Saturated Fat 4.9g Cholesterol 20mg Sodium 63mg Carbohydrate 26.2g Dietary Fiber 4.5g Sugars 15.1g Protein 2.8g Calcium 67mg Phosphorous 105mg Potassium 170mg

Apple Cinnamon Pie

Cooking time: 50 minutes

Servings: 12

Ingredients: Apple Filling:

9 cups apples, peeled, cored and sliced

1 tablespoon stevia

1/3 cup all-purpose flour

2 tablespoons lemon juice

1 teaspoon ground cinnamon

2 tablespoons butter

Pie Dough:

2 1/4 cups all-purpose flour

1 teaspoon stevia

1 1/2 sticks unsalted butter

6 oz. cream cheese

3 tablespoons cold heavy whipping cream

Water, if needed

Direction:

Start by preheating your gas oven at 425 degrees F.

Mix the apple slices with cinnamon, 1 tablespoon of butter, lemon juice, flour and stevia in a bowl and keep it aside covered.

Whisk the flour with stevia, butter, cream cheese and cream in mixing bowl to form the dough.

If the dough is too dry, slowly add some water to make a smooth dough ball.

Cut the dough into two equal-size pieces and spread them into a 9-inch sheet.

Place one of the sheets at the bottom of a 9-inch pie pan.

Evenly spread the apples in this pie shell and add a tablespoon of butter over it.

Cover the apple filling with the second sheet of the dough and pinch down the edges.

Make 1-inch deep cuts on top of the pie and bake for about 50 minutes until golden.

Slice and serve.

Nutritional information per serving: *Calories 303*

Total Fat 8.8g Saturated Fat 5.3g Cholesterol 26mg Sodium 30mg Carbohydrate 21.7g Dietary Fiber 4.8g Sugars 19.6g

Protein 4.2g Calcium 21mg Phosphorous 381mg Potassium 229mg

Maple Crisp Bars

Cooking time: 5 minutes

Servings: 20

Ingredients:

1/3 cup butter

1 cup brown Swerve

1 teaspoon maple extract

1/2 cup maple syrup

8 cups puffed rice cereal

Direction:

Mix the butter with Swerve, maple extract, and syrup in a saucepan over moderate heat.

Cook by slowly stirring this mixture for 5 minutes then toss in the rice cereal.

Mix well, then press this cereal mixture in a 13x9 inches baking dish.

Refrigerate the mixture for 2 hours then cut into 20 bars.

Serve.

Nutritional information per serving: *Calories 107*

Total Fat 3.1g Saturated Fat 0.5g Cholesterol 0mg Sodium 36mg Carbohydrate 10.6g Dietary Fiber 0.1g Sugars 5.4g Protein 0.4g Calcium 7mg Phosphorous 233mg Potassium 24mg

Chapter 15: 21-Day Kidney Diet Plan

DAY	BREAKFAST	LUNCH/DINNER	SNACK/DESSERT
1.	Cottage Cheese Pancakes	Chicken Noodle Soup	Cream Cheese Tarts
2.	Asparagus Bacon Hash	Beef Stew with Apple Cider	Orange Biscotti
3.	Pineapple Bread	Chicken Chili	Strawberry Delight
4.	Parmesan Zucchini Frittata	Lamb Stew	Lemon Squares
5.	Cheese Spaghetti Frittata	Tofu Stir Fry	Creamy Pineapple Dessert
6.	Texas Toast Casserole	Broccoli Pancake	
7.	Apple Cinnamon Rings	Carrot Casserole	Blackberry Mountain Pie

8.	Zucchini Bread	Cauliflower Rice	Buttery Lemon Squares
9.	Garlic Mayo Bread	Chicken Pineapple Curry	Chocolate Gelatin Mousse
10.	Strawberry Topped Waffles	Baked Pork Chops	Blackberry Cream Cheese Pie
11.	Mixed Pepper Mushroom Omelet	Lasagna Rolls In Marinara Sauce	Apple Cinnamon Pie
12.	Simple Zucchini BBQ	Chicken Curry	Maple Crisp Bars
13.	Bacon and Chicken Garlic Wrap	Steak with Onion	Winter Berry Smoothie
14.	Angel Eggs	Lemon Pepper Trout	Carrot Smoothie
15.	Omelet	Salmon Stuffed Pasta	Strawberry Papaya Smoothie

16.	Blackberry Pudding	Tuna Casserole	Gut Cleansing Smoothie
17.	Simple Green Shake	Oregano Salmon with Crunchy Crust	Cabbage and Chia Glass
18.	Green Beans and Roasted Onion	Sardine Fish Cakes	Blueberry and Kale Mix
19.	Fine Morning Porridge	Cajun Catfish	Cucumber and Pineapple Smoothie
20.	Hungarian's Porridge	Teriyaki Tuna	Raspberry Smoothie
21.	Awesome Nut Porridge	Herbed Vegetable Trout	Protein Peach Smoothie

LOW-SODIUM SLOW COOKER

Chapter 16: Low sodium diet overview.

We all know that overeating salt is bad or us but what's the problem, exactly?

This is a cookbook, and so I am not going to bore you with pages and pages of science. This simple overview will give you the general picture as to why we should cut down on salt and the damage it can do to our bodies.

First and foremost, salt raises the blood pressure in our bodies, and this has various effects and manifestations for our health.

How Much Sodium Should You Consume?

Current recommendations are that Americans should eat around 1500-2300mg of sodium per day. But you can easily exceed your daily recommended amount just by having a breakfast cereal and lunch at a fast-food restaurant.

The problem with salt is it makes things taste great, and it's cheap. Manufacturers and fast food giants literally lace food with cheap salt. Sadly, they clearly care more about fat profits rather than the health of their customers.

However, with the recipes in this book, you'll find it easy to stick to these recommendations. And by aiming for a lower daily amount of sodium in your diet, you can expect to see results fast. In fact, your blood pressure can reduce in just two weeks.

Damaged Arteries

When your blood pressure is raised, this puts a strain on our arteries. And it's harder to pump the blood around our bodies. As a result, if you have had raised blood pressure for some time, your arteries will have to adapt to the job they need to do. They become stronger and thicker. But this is not a good thing because the space in the arteries become narrower.

Thus, it just makes your blood pressure even higher as blood is pumped through a smaller space. Eventually, the arteries either burst or clog – and then you have a big problem. The organs don't receive the nutrients they need; they become damaged, and often the result is fatal.

If the artery in question which bursts or becomes clogs is in the heart, then the result is a heart attack. A reduction in the blood reaching the heart results in frightening and painful angina.

If the artery in question is in your brain, then a reduction in blood supply can lead to dementia while a clot or blockage leads to a stroke.

I think it's fair to say that many of us will have witnessed first-hand, possibly with grandparents the devastation of such conditions. And obviously, everyone wants to avoid this life-changing, dangerous, and fatal health implications for themselves.

The great news is you can! And you can still eat great, tasty food.

As long as you are not eating processed and fast food, you should be able to reach your recommended daily amount reasonably easily. There are so many foods on this potassium-rich list that I would challenge even the pickiest eater not to be able to make significant health changes.

Vegetables All vegetables will give you a potassium boost, but these are some of the most potassium-rich ones.

Potatoes (One medium baked potato delivers a massive 941mg of potassium! It's the perfect accompaniment to many of the slow-cooker meat stews and dishes in this book – and is a far tastier and healthier option than sodium packed and low potassium burger meal with fries).

Broccoli

Sweet potatoes

Mushrooms

Peas

Cucumbers

Zucchini

Eggplant

Pumpkins

Leafy greens (you can easily get over 800mg of potassium in a 1 cup serving of spinach or other greens such as Swiss Chard).

Tomatoes (tomatoes are easy to add to many dishes, and just ½ cup of tomato puree contains around 500mg of potassium).

Fruit

Bananas (just one banana contains over 400mg of potassium and is a filling and healthy snack).

Oranges

Cantaloupe

Honeydew

Apricots (just ½ cup of dried apricots makes a sweet snack full of fiber and contain over 1,100mg of potassium).

Grapefruit

Dried fruits, such as prunes, raisins, and dates (1/2 cup of prunes with your breakfast oatmeal or cereal delivers around 700mg of potassium).

Fish A small 3-oz serving of the following fish packs a mighty potassium punch. You can even double up and have a 6-oz serve for double the potassium goodness:

Atlantic Salmon 534 mg

Mackerel: 474 mg

Halibut: 449 mg

Snapper: 444 mg

Rainbow trout: 383 mg

Beans or legumes that are high in potassium include: 1 cup of beans contains the following amount of potassium:

Kidney beans 607mg

Lima beans 478mg

Adzuki beans: 612 mg

Cannellini beans: 595 mg

Black beans: 401 mg

Canned refried beans: 380 mg

Lentils (if you like lentils then just 1 cup will deliver over 700g of potassium).

Other foods that are rich in potassium include: Certain dairy products, such as milk and yogurt, are high in potassium. Choose low-fat options to keep cholesterol levels down.

Lower sodium levels and higher potassium levels can also improve the effectiveness of any blood pressure medications that your physician has prescribed.

It is absolutely possible and to be expected to make significant improvements to your health stats in just a few weeks.

Maybe more so than in any other types of patients, there is far less upheaval for patients aiming to reduce their blood pressure by cutting their sodium levels than say, for example, a diabetic patient cutting carbohydrate.

And, many patients prefer their new style of eating and cooking. Instead of just adding too much salt and very little thought, they finally begin to experiment with delicious flavor-packed herbs and spices – and love the results!

How Can a Low Sodium and Salt Diet Help You?

When you think of sodium in your diet, particularly added sodium, more than likely the first thought that pops into your head is table salt. Unfortunately for you, table salt is the least of your worries when it comes to added sodium, although it certainly is the easiest sodium level to control.

Sodium is necessary. While it is present in salt, which is a seasoning that most people love, it is also very helpful to your body. Without sodium, our bodies would not be able to regulate our fluids, keep our electrolytes balanced, keep our cells functioning, or maintain our blood pressure (Kubala, 2018).

To start your new lifestyle, you will need to limit your sodium to less than 2,300 mg (2.3 grams) of salt, which is around 2 teaspoons of salt a day (Kubala, 2018).

Do not think of your new lifestyle change as a restriction or a *diet*. Think of it as a return to what you should have been eating all along. Imagine if you had always eaten a bowl of chocolate ice cream with caramel syrup, whipped cream, and

Oreo cookies on top every single morning for breakfast. And every single afternoon, you were sick to your stomach. Until one day, you decided to stop eating that giant bowl of ice cream with all of those toppings. You may have craved the ice cream later, but you didn't feel physically sick. You were going back to normal.

Think of your new low sodium diet as a method of reverting back to your body's actual needs, in terms of sodium levels. Most people consume far more sodium (and salt) than they need for their bodies to function properly. Without proper levels of sodium, your body cannot regulate the amount of fluid you have in your body, contract your muscles, send out nerve impulses, and regulate your blood pressure (Mozaffarian, n.d.).

Maintaining Your Sodium Levels

Part of maintaining a healthy diet and a healthy body is properly maintaining your sodium levels. When your levels are not maintained properly, you could suffer from hyponatremia or hypernatremia.

Hyponatremia

Hyponatremia literally means that the sodium levels present in your blood are too low. One of the ways that you can develop this condition—which causes your body's cells to swell—is by drinking too much water. In more serious, life-threatening cases, you will have to receive electrolyte solutions intravenously ("Hyponatremia", n.d.).

If you suspect that you have hyponatremia, look for the following symptoms: muscle weakness or cramps, confusion, vomiting/nausea, low to no energy, constant fatigue, and headaches. Watch out for these symptoms, particularly if you start vomiting, cramping, and have frequent headaches ("Hyponatremia", n.d.).

There are several causes behind hyponatremia. The most common cause is drinking too much water, which overwhelms the kidney's function to excrete water vs sodium, but there are several other causes you may be familiar with—congestive heart failure, kidney failure, severe dehydration through excessive vomiting and/or diarrhea, and the use of any anti-diuretic hormones. All of these causes will ensure that your body holds onto the fluid it has already filtered so that it stays in your body ("Hyponatremia", n.d.).

This condition has two stages. The chronic version can sneak up on you over a period of 48 hours, and mainly gives you moderate symptoms. However, the acute version occurs all at once, causing your sodium levels to drop almost instantaneously. If you are not careful, your brain could swell and this could even be fatal ("Hyponatremia", n.d.). Pay close attention to any symptoms you may have experienced in the past as you begin your journey to a healthier life.

Women who are close to the perimenopausal stage seem to be at a much higher risk of hyponatremia, as their sex hormones are linked to how the body balances sodium levels ("Hyponatremia", n.d.).

Hypernatremia

Hypernatremia literally means that the sodium levels present in your blood are too high. Sometimes you can get away with mild hypernatremia, without affecting your health (McBean, 2017). However, if you do not get it under control you could end up in serious trouble.

If you suspect that you have hypernatremia at any moment, look for the following symptoms: lethargy (usually presenting as low to no energy and severe fatigue), extreme thirst, and, sometimes, confusion. In more rare cases, you may suffer from spasms *e.g.* muscle twitching. This is due to the fact that your sodium levels influence how your nerves and muscles work (McBean, 2017).

You will have a higher chance of developing hypernatremia if you already suffer from diabetes, kidney disease, dehydration, vomiting, diarrhea (if it is watery), and several other conditions (McBean, 2017).

Be careful—hypernatremia is an acute condition that can strike you within a day. The most important aspect of treatment is to correct the sodium and fluid balance in your body. More than likely, your fluid intake will be increased and then your sodium levels will be checked. Also, something to consider—hypernatremia is usually an underlying condition and a symptom of a bigger problem (McBean, 2017).

Tips on Cooking Low-Sodium Meals

Now let's take a look at "sodium culprits". And how by following my quick and easy changes to your diet, you will dramatically reduce your sodium intake. And thus, rapidly improve your health.

1 Table & Cooking Salt First of all, simply throw out your regular salt and replace with a low-sodium salt. One teaspoon of salt contains 2300mg of sodium. That's about the top level you should be aiming to consume for one day. But simply changing to a low-sodium salt alternative will cut that in half!

2 Taste your food the majority of people add salt to their food at the table. Now, that's fine if you have followed the first tip and have swapped to low-sodium salt. But I would still offer a few more tips here.

Now, many top-level chefs perfectly season and taste the food they prepare before it is served to you. Many of these chefs do not account for personal taste or differing taste buds. But consider customers that salt the food they have prepared, without first tasting it, as the height of bad manners and disrespect.

I, too, cook for people that pick up the salt shaker without ever tasting it, and I admit to a certain level of annoyance. So, first of all, it's not necessary to ban salt at the table but please, please, please, taste your food first and get out of the salt-everything-first-habit.

Stop and take a few bites to taste what is in your plate before you cover your food in salt. Taste, the meat, the potatoes, the vegetables and assess what the food tastes like first. Especially now that you are trying out new flavors and spices in your food, it might be that you don't need to add any salt. Or maybe just the potatoes are a little under seasoned for your taste.

3 Change your Salt Shaker If you are a person that always adds salt to your food at the table, then consider investing a few dollars in a new salt shaker. What you are looking for in a new salt shaker is one that dispenses salt at a slower rate. Salt shakers tend to have larger holes than pepper shakers for larger salt crystals. But often they send salt pouring out of the shaker at quite an alarming rate. It's usually very easy to over-salt your food and add it far too liberally.

4 Measure Salt at the Table Without getting caught up in stereotypes of domestic life, it can often be that one person is cooking the food in the home for the person that needs to reduce their sodium levels. So, after a loved one spends hours in the kitchen carefully measuring out low-sodium salt and flavorings. It's not particularly fair to undo all their hard work by just adding as much salt at the table, as though nothing mattered.

Now, I am not suggesting that you start measuring out quarter teaspoons of salt at the table. However, what you can do is measure out or use a pre-bought small salt shaker with a known amount of low-sodium salt. Typically, that might be 2 ounces or 50g or ten teaspoons. You'll be tasting your food by now, if you are following tip two on my list, so see how long it takes you to use an easy-to-measure amount of salt. You might mark a line halfway down your salt shaker that lets you know when you have consumed ten teaspoons of salt. This way you will know exactly how much salt you are adding at the table. And if this is an area you still need to watch.

5 *Garlic Lovers* I happen to love garlic as do many people, and I know a lot of salt-addicts also adore garlic salt. Garlic salt can be sprinkled on most food if you love garlic, of course – whether it's meat and fish, soups, stews, carbohydrates or vegetables. Make your own garlic salt to add to your food by using one-part low-sodium salt to two parts garlic granules. A one-quarter teaspoon serving of salt will come in at around 600mg of sodium. And it's a quarter of the maximum amount you should be aiming for in a day. Your low-sodium

garlic salt quarter teaspoon serving will have just 100mg of sodium so you can afford to add a little extra.

6 Other Alternatives The amount of salt in pre-packaged US food means it can be tough for Americans to buy regular food without it being laced with salt. There is salt in desserts, cakes, breakfast cereals, and just about everything you could think of. However, in addition to that, the US market is also renowned for giving Americans unrivaled consumer choice.

7 Eating Out There's no need to stop dining out just because you need to follow a low-sodium diet. Follow a couple of tips and you can eat out several times a week.

i) Many family chain restaurants produce heart-healthy meals clearly indicated on their menus. They have carefully counted and labeled levels of fat, cholesterol, and sodium. Simply choose those!

ii) If you are dining in shall we say more sophisticated restaurants, then inform your server that you are on a low-sodium diet. And ask for your meal to be prepared without salt. Then salt your own meal with your brought along low-sodium salt shaker.

iii) Fast food restaurants are typically not the best place to frequent as most of the food is packed with cheap salt. But you can still order fries that are unsalted and burgers just plain with salad. Then add your own low-sodium ketchup, mayo, barbeque, and burger sauce. Do remember though that fries are still fried so are not the most heart-healthy food. So, keep these visits to treats and infrequent occasions.

8 Curry Love The ultimate in tasty flavorsome food has to be curry. If you love curries, then my advice is to get experimenting. The flavor in curries comes from gently cooking blends of spices with onion and garlic for a fantastic base.

9 Preparation You'll note that some of the recipes in this book include canned beans and vegetables. It's a far lower calorie option. But often the only option to have these types of produce preserved in brine or saltwater. Beans and vegetables are a heart-healthy food, but what about the salt in the brine?

Well, the good news is that laboratory analysis proves that rinsing the produce well can cut the sodium content by a quarter. So, don't miss out on fat-free filling foods that are great for the heart.

Chapter 17: Operation and tricks for the slow cooker. What not to do.

It's time to rethink that. Slow cookers are a great tool for making healthy meals with minimal fuss. How?

Versatility

Fresh vegetables, a variety of potatoes and winter squash, and pretty much any cut of meat work very well in the slow cooker. Slow cookers let you use less expensive ingredients. For example, using dry beans and just soaking them overnight is not only healthier but cheaper, too.

Minimal prep

Throw the ingredients in and let them cook—that's the slow cooker way! Not only will you save time, but you will have a lot fewer pots and pans to clean up as well. The recipes here are great for when you need to clean out your produce drawer, too—grab your veggies, chop them up, and throw them into the slow cooker.

Cook and freeze

If you want or need to make your meals in advance, most of the recipes in this book are freezer-friendly. If you spend a couple hours prepping freezer meals for the week, you'll be more likely to keep your low-sodium diet on track.

Great flavor, better texture

A slow cooker brings out the flavor in foods—so much flavor, in fact, that you can cook with a lot less salt and sugar. Slow cooking also delivers melt-in-your-mouth meat! The low and slow method of the slow cooker produces meat so tender you can shred it with a fork. The best part is that even the cheapest, toughest cuts of meat will cook up tender and delicious.

Maximize the nutrients

Cooking food at low temperatures for a long time preserves nutrients that are normally lost when food is cooked at high temperatures. Slow cooking also eliminates the risk of ages (advanced glycation end products), which form when foods are cooked at high heat and are known to contribute to increased oxidative stress and inflammation, which have been linked to diabetes and cardiovascular disease.

Avoid temptation

When you throw everything in your slow cooker in the morning and head out for work, you know you're going to come home to a cooked meal (and probably an amazing-smelling house). This will help you avoid eating out or stopping for takeout as often—thus avoiding all the temptations of a restaurant menu.

Slow Cooking Tips and Tricks

While slow cooking is a very easy technique, there are a few tips and tricks you'll need to keep in mind: • Chop food in large chunks, particularly vegetables and potatoes. This will keep them from falling apart when they get very soft.

• Make sure to cut the meat and vegetables into pieces that are all about the same size, so they cook evenly.

• Cut to fit. If your roast is too big, cut it into two pieces. Do the same for vegetables and even noodles.

• Use frozen vegetables by layering appropriately. Place firm root vegetables (think potatoes) at the bottom of the slow cooker, then the meat, then the frozen vegetables on top.

• Don't remove the lid; set it and forget it. Lifting the lid releases heat—so much that you have to add as much as 30 minutes additional cooking time just from taking a quick peek!

• Don't overcrowd the slow cooker. This will lead to food cooking unevenly or not all the way through.

• Ditch the premade dressing, sauce, and seasoning packets and make your own. You can do this easily, using simple seasonings and spices that you probably already have in your pantry. (You'll find some examples below.) Same flavor, way less sodium.

• To brown or not to brown the meat before you add it to the slow cooker? Some people argue that it adds flavor. I'm not 100 percent convinced that's the case, so I usually think of any browning or searing as an optional step.

Slow Cookers & The Low-Sodium Cook

Slow cookers have many benefits in particular for those wanting to cut down on sodium. You know yourself that when you cook things for longer, the flavors have more time to develop. But we don't all have the time to stand around, stirring the food for hours. The slow cooker solves that problem. You can just walk away and allow the slow cooker to do its thing as those robust and rounded flavors develop.

When you use a slow cooker, the meat and vegetables have so much longer to take on the flavors of the herbs, spices, and broths you add. The flavor of the meat and vegetables amalgamate and become more intensified - and that's a great boon when you want to prepare fuller flavored dishes but with much less salt.

Not just that, typically, tougher cuts of meat are more flavorsome than quicker cooking cuts. When the meat fibers break down, you'll have delicious melt-in-the-mouth meat – and at a fraction of the price.

A slow cooker also has many other benefits. Even though a slow cooker is turned on for a longer time, they are more economical than other ways of cooking. So, you'll be helping to save the planet, in addition to making tasty, healthy meals.

What I also love is the fact that often you can just add the ingredients to the slow cooker in the morning with virtually no mess. And when you return in the evening after a long hard day at the office – your home is filled with delicious aromas, and your dinner is hot and ready to serve.

Slow Cooker Do's & Don'ts

Do: Make sure your cable is not underneath the slow cooker when cooking as this is a fire hazard.

Do: Read the manual Do: Try not to lift the lid too often! Follow the recipe and stir as advised only otherwise you will let the heat out and slow down the desired cooking time.

Do: Check the recipe and use the right size slow cooker.

Do: Follow the recipe and layer the meat and vegetables as advised so that vegetables are at the bottom and have longer to cook than the meat.

Do: Brown meat as advised in the recipe as a slow cooker can't caramelize your meat and give it that extra flavor.

Do: Use lean meats in your recipe so that you are following low fat and a heart-healthy diet. Drain off any fat as advised in the recipe.

Do: Make sure the slow cooker is cool before you wash it to prevent it from cracking.

Do: Add tender vegetables, seafood, pasta, dairy products, and fresh herbs toward the end of cooking as advised in the recipe to prevent the food from becoming overcooked or from curdling.

Do: Use wooden, plastic, and rubber utensils when you stir.

Do: Cut vegetables such as sweet potatoes, carrot, swede, and potatoes evenly so that can cook evenly.

Don't: Put your slow cooker in the fridge. The ceramic pot is not designed to withstand cold temperatures and may crack. Empty leftover contents into fridge-safe containers and store covered. You can also freeze many dishes and reheat later.

Don't: Use your slow cooker to reheat food. The slow cooker is a cooker and is not designed to reach the correct temperatures to reheat food safely. Reheat leftover meals in a microwave, in a conventional oven, or a saucepan.

Don't: Cook food from frozen. Always use food that has been thawed to ensure that food is heated to the right temperature. Because the slow cooker heats the food slowly it can cause bacteria to grow, don't: Be afraid to experiment and try new things with your slow cooker. You can adapt your favorite recipes to cook in your slow cooker with a little thought.

Don't: Be afraid of cornflour. If your meal looks a little watery, then simply remove the lid and stir in some cornflour to thicken the sauce.

Don't: Overfill your pot. If you add too many ingredients and fill your slow cooker to the brim, it may have a hard time cooking it. You may return home after 8 hours to find the food is still not cooked as there isn't enough power to cook all the food through.

Flavoring the Low-Sodium Way

At first, sticking to a low-sodium diet can make seasoning difficult. You're not adding salt, and many store-bought products, like seasoning packets and dressings, are high in sodium. The answer is to make them yourself. I think you'll find that their homemade replacements are just as good, if not better.

Herbs, whether fresh or dried, and more unusual spices like curry or basic seasonings like cumin, can do wonders for a dish. The combination possibilities are endless, and you can tailor the flavors to your tastes. Like spicy? Make chili powder your base for a nice, spicy blend. Homemade blends add so much flavor, all without any added sodium.

Chapter 18: Sodium consumption: how to balance consumption and how much you should consume.

Foods with High Levels of Sodium

As stated earlier in this eBook, your daily sodium intake should be closer to 2,300 mg (or 2.3 grams) or 1 teaspoon of salt a day. This is particularly important to abide by if you suffer from heart disease, high blood pressure, or kidney failure.

However, there are several foods that are naturally high in sodium that you should avoid, or consume less of, and there are also foods that contain a surprising amount of sodium that perhaps you had never considered as a significant source of sodium. The following is a general list of sodium high foods, however, when you buy any food product you should read the label or use an online search engine to figure out how much sodium is in what you're holding, per serving.

Per serving is key. One fried chicken mini drumstick could have 1,150 mg of sodium, which would appear to be good as that is exactly half of the amount of sodium you should (generally) be consuming. However, a mini drumstick is barely larger than your thumb and there is no way you would only eat *two* of those as a meal.

Shrimp

The first surprising addition - shrimp. Even if you buy plain shrimp in the frozen packages, you still need to read the Nutrition: Often, "plain" frozen shrimp is actually lightly salted and then bathed in sodium heavy preservatives before the freezing process. A 3-ounce bag could contain as much as 800 mg of sodium. If you have the choice, go for freshly caught shrimp, or buy frozen shrimp that does not have salt additives (McCulloch, 2018).

Ham and Sausage

Sausage is naturally very fatty, so it is no surprise that it leads the pack with 415 mg of sodium within 2-ounce servings. Another easy to see example is ham. Ham often ends up extremely salty and high in sodium because salt is used to preserve, cure, and flavor the meat. That is why for every 3-ounce serving of ham you get, you will be eating 1,117 mg of sodium (McCulloch, 2018).

Canned Soup and Meat

Any sort of prepackaged soup will often have a high percentage of sodium, the sodium is used as a component of the preservation process.

Canned meats *e.g.* tuna, chicken, turkey have also been gaining a lot of attention due to the amount of sodium they've been found to contain. Some brands have used as much as 425 mg of sodium per 3 ounce/single serving, which is incredibly high (McCulloch, 2018).

Cottage Cheese

While cottage cheese is a wonderful source of protein and calcium, it is very high in salt compared to the other two. A regular ½ cup serving size is the equivalent of eating 350 mg of salt a day. You will not see any reduced or no-sodium versions of cottage cheese, as unfortunately the salt not only alters the taste and texture of the product itself but is also a preserving agent for the cottage cheese. However, it has been shown that if you run cold water over your cottage cheese, then you can reduce the amount of sodium present by around (McCulloch, 2018).

Vegetable Juice

While it may seem extra healthy to you, commercially available vegetable juices are often some of the worst offenders for high sodium levels present in foodstuffs. Pay attention to the nutrition labels of what you're consuming, especially if you think it's healthy. It never hurts to double-check. The healthy vegetable juice that you are drinking might have 5 or 6 different kinds of vegetable juice in it, but it could also have 405 mg of sodium per serving and 3.5 servings in the entire bottle. If you still want to drink commercially available vegetable juice, make sure that you buy reduced-sodium versions. Legally, the sodium levels cannot be higher than 140 mg per serving (McCulloch, 2018).

Salad Dressing

While some salad dressing contains higher sodium levels due to salt actually added to the dressings themselves for flavor, the biggest culprit is the type of salad dressings that have additives with sodium in them *e.g.* MSG, disodium inosinate, *etc.* (McCulloch, 2018). Be careful of the salad dressing that you choose if you still buy them after reading this eBook. Always go with the reduced or sodium-free options if you can. Otherwise, be aware that the majority of salad dressings average between 304 mg per 2 tablespoon serving (McCulloch, 2018).

Broth and Sauces

As we have established, sodium is an ingredient not only used in preserving, but flavorings as well. However, the use of sodium as a flavoring has gone a bit too far, for far too long. For example, an 8-ounce serving of a simple beef broth contains 782 mg of sodium. To combat this, either make your own broth and sauces or buy explicitly marked low or reduced-sodium broths and sauces (McCulloch, 2018).

Canned Vegetables

Again, as part of the preservation process, canned vegetables have more than their own fair share of sodium, with an average ½ cup serving size containing 310 mg of sodium. Luckily, if you drain and then rinse your canned vegetables in cool water for a few minutes, then you can reduce the amount of sodium that you are eating by at least (McCulloch, 2018). If you don't want to deal with the sodium issue at all, then you can buy fresh or frozen vegetables.

Consequences of Excess Sodium

As stated earlier in this eBook, when you have high levels of sodium, that means your body is taking in more sodium than it needs or can handle. A small amount of extra sodium won't make a big difference in your overall health, but very often these types of situations escalate. If you continue to consume an excess of sodium, then your sodium levels will continue to rise, and your taste buds will become used to the processed, over-salted foods. Eventually, it will all come out in your health.

Your health will always tell the tale when it comes to your sodium levels. Perhaps you suffer symptoms of hypernatremia, high blood pressure, kidney disease, or heart failure. You may not know what those symptoms are, per se, but you will understand that something is wrong.

Symptoms of Hypernatremia

As covered before, hypernatremia (higher than normal levels of sodium) provides you with several symptoms to hint at its existence, the first being extreme thirst. What you may not know is that this could get ugly pretty fast, if your case is severe enough. If you worsen and do not seek medical attention or change your diet, then you could have issues communicating or even end up not being able to get your own water (Lewis, 2018). The next symptom is confusion, and in the worst case, you can end up slipping into a coma. The confusion is an outward manifestation of your brain cells literally shrinking, as your brain cells are dehydrated (Lewis, 2018).

Diagnosis of this condition is usually straightforward—in a hospital setting, your sodium levels would be measured. If your levels are measured to be high, then you will be given water orally, and if your levels do not change after a certain period of time, further testing would be needed. However, the main treatment is just that--introducing more fluids into your body. An acute (sudden) case of hypernatremia should settle itself within 24 hours. Otherwise, you will need an extended hospital stay (Lewis, 2018).

Symptoms of High Blood Pressure

High blood pressure occurs when the amount of blood that your arteries pump is elevated or when your arteries become too narrow. Your blood pressure rises, which can cause long-term stress to your artery walls, resulting in a stroke or heart attack. Unfortunately, you can go for years without any symptoms of high blood pressure, which is why it is vital that you change your diet now, even if you aren't currently experiencing any symptoms ("High Blood Pressure", n.d.).

As stated above, the vast majority of people who have high blood pressure do not experience any symptoms, that is to say, they do not experience any of the recognizable symptoms of high blood pressure. This is normal, even if your blood pressure is a record-setting high. However, some people have reported symptoms such as nosebleeds, shortness of breath, and headaches—however, these symptoms did not occur until shortly before the person experienced a stroke or heart attack ("High Blood Pressure", n.d.).

The best way to diagnose or monitor your blood pressure is to get your blood pressure taken regularly. You can even buy a blood pressure cuff to take home with you and take your own blood pressure. If you have a family history involving heart attacks or strokes, it might not be a bad idea to either get your blood pressure taken regularly if you do not already, or take it regularly yourself, as you start this new journey.

Symptoms of Kidney Disease

Kidney disease is more commonly known as acute kidney failure. This occurs when your kidneys are just not able to filter your blood anymore. The effect of your kidneys not being able to filter your blood anymore means that any waste that it would have filtered out previously, such as excess sodium, is trapped in your body. The majority of the time, kidney failure is irreversible, even in sudden cases ("Acute Kidney Failure", n.d.).

Symptoms of kidney disease are relatively straightforward— if you suffer from, first and foremost, a huge reduction in the amount you pee, although you can occasionally go normally, and fluid retention, particularly in your ankles, legs, or feet, then you may have kidney disease. Couple this with the following symptoms—fatigue, nausea, weakness, confusion, chest pain, shortness of breath, and so on ("Acute Kidney Failure", n.d.).

If you have ever suffered from kidney disease due to eating an increased level of high sodium foods over a long (or short) period of time, then the obvious treatment is to increase your fluid (water) intake. However, if your case is particularly difficult, then you may need to take your fluids intravenously, and perhaps take a diuretic to allow you to expel the waste (excess sodium) ("Acute Kidney Failure", n.d.). With a proper diet, this would not happen at all.

Symptoms of Heart Failure

Heart failure seems to be a dirty word among the three other symptoms or hints that may point to you having higher than healthy levels of sodium. Heart failure is categorized as the heart's inability to pump blood throughout the arteries and veins of your body at the same level it operated at previously. The only way that you can prevent heart failure is to control the risk factors that can lead to heart failure, which include diabetes, high blood pressure, coronary artery disease, and obesity ("Heart Failure", n.d.).

The symptoms that point directly at heart failure include edema (swelling in legs, feet, and ankles), fluid retention, shortness of breath whenever you change positions (lay down or sit up), fatigue, increased urinary output, and chest pain ("Heart Failure", n.d.).

Part of the diagnosis of heart failure includes checking whether or not you have high blood pressure ("Heart Failure", n.d.). High blood pressure is a great contributing factor to heart failure, and a reduction of sodium intake followed by an increased fluid intake is the only thing that will lower your blood pressure, and in turn, lower your chances of heart failure.

Chapter 19: Breakfast

Apple Cinnamon Oatmeal

Servings: 2

Preparation time 5 m

Cooking time: *10 m*

ingredients

1 c water

1/4 c apple juice

1 apple, cored and chopped

2/3 c rolled oats

1 tsp. ground cinnamon

1 c milk

Directions

In a saucepan over high heat, mix the apple juice, apples, and water together. Let the mixture boil. Add the cinnamon and rolled oats. Stir and allow to boil again. Adjust heat to low to simmer for around 3 minutes until the oatmeal is thick. Use a spoon to transfer the oatmeal into serving bowls. Pour milk over the oatmeal before serving.

Nutrition:

Calories: 217

Total Fat: 4.3 g

Carbohydrates: 38.1g

Protein: 7.8 g

Cholesterol: 10 mg

Sodium: 57 mg

Autumn Apple Salad

Servings: 4

Preparation time 10 m

Cooking time: *10 m*

ingredients

4 tart green apples, cored and chopped

1/4 c blanched slivered almonds, toasted

1/4 c dried cranberries

1/4 c chopped dried cherries

1 (8 ounce) container vanilla yogurt

Directions

Combine the cranberries, apples, yogurt, cherries, and almonds in a medium-sized bowl. Stir until the mixture is coated evenly.

Nutrition:

Calories: 202

Total fat: 4.1 g

Carbohydrates: 38.9g

Protein: 5.1 g

Cholesterol: 3 mg <

Sodium: 41 mg

Banana, chocolate, and almond breakfast oatmeal

Servings: 2

Preparation time 10 m

Cooking time: *15 m*

ingredients

1 c milk

1/4 c unsweetened cocoa powder

2 1/2 tbsps. Turbinado sugar

1/2 tsp. Almond extract

1 large banana, slightly mashed

1/2 c quick cooking oats

1/4 c blanched slivered almonds

Directions

In a saucepan over medium-low heat, whisk together the turbinado sugar, almond extract, milk, and cocoa powder. When the sugar dissolves, let the mixture simmer.

Add the oatmeal and mashed banana and stir. Simmer for around 5 minutes until the banana has partially broken, and the oatmeal has become thick. Fold the almonds into the oatmeal before serving.

Nutrition:

Calories: 366

Total fat: 12.3 g

Carbohydrates: 58.4g

Protein: 12.4 g

Cholesterol: 10 mg

Sodium: 62 mg

Banana nut oatmeal

Servings: 1

preparation time 5 m

Cooking time: 7 m

ingredients

1/4 c quick cooking oats

1/2 c skim milk

1 tsp. Flax seeds

2 tbsps. Chopped walnuts

3 tbsps. Honey

1 banana, peeled

Directions

In a microwave-safe bowl, mix together the flax seeds, oats, banana milk, honey, and walnuts. Set the microwave on high and cook for 2 minutes. Use a fork to mash the banana. Then stir in the mashed banana to the mixture. Serve immediately.

Nutrition:

Calories: 532

Total fat: 13.1 g

Carbohydrates: 101.7g

Protein: 11.2 g

Cholesterol: 2 mg <

Sodium: 58 mg

Beer batter crepes

Servings: 12

preparation time 1 m

Cooking time: *1 h 15 m*

ingredients

3 eggs, lightly beaten

1 c milk

1 c beer

1 3/4 c all-purpose flour

1 pinch salt

2 tbsps. Vegetable oil

2 tbsps. Butter

Directions

Whisk beer, milk, and eggs together in a big bowl. Whisk in flour slowly and add the oil and salt. Whisk the batter strongly until thoroughly blended for 3 to 5 minutes. Leave the batter for an hour.

Place a 10-inch, nonstick skillet over medium heat and then brush it with butter. When the skillet is already hot (but not smoking), put a one-third c of batter into the middle portion.

Turn the skillet to make the batter cover the bottom in a thin layer. Remove any excess batter. Cook for a minute or two. When the crepe becomes golden on one side, turn it and cook for half a minute until golden. Place each crepe on a plate and cover with foil to keep it warm. Do this step again until you've used up all the batter.

Nutrition:

Calories: 140

Total fat: 6 g

Carbohydrates: 15.7g

Protein: 4.2 g

Cholesterol: 53 mg

Sodium: 41 mg

Best bircher muesli

Servings: 4

Preparation time 5 m

Cooking time: *8 h 5 m*

ingredients

2 c rolled oats

3 tbsps. Raisins

3 tbsps. Honey

1 1/2 c plain yogurt

1 1/4 c soy milk

Directions

Combine the honey, soy milk, oats, yogurt, and raisins in a big glass bowl. Cover the bowl and place in the fridge. Chill it overnight. Serve.

Nutrition:

Calories: 323

Total fat: 5.4 g

Carbohydrates: 57.8g

Protein: 12.9 g

Cholesterol: 6 mg

Sodium: 107 mg

Swiss oatmeal

Servings: 4

Preparation time 15 m

Cooking time: *1 h 15 m*

ingredients

2 c rolled oats

1 green apple, chopped

1 c milk

1 c nonfat plain yogurt

1 banana, chopped

1/4 c raisins

1 tbsp. Chopped walnuts

1 tbsp. Slivered almonds

1 tbsp. Brown sugar

1 tbsp. Honey

1 tbsp. Orange juice

Directions

In a bowl, combine brown sugar, milk, orange juice, oats, honey, almonds, walnuts, apple, banana, raisins, and yogurt. Refrigerate until set for at least 60 minutes or more.

Nutrition:

Calories: 344

Total fat: 6.2 g

Carbohydrates: 62.8g

Protein: 12.3 g

Cholesterol: 6 mg

Sodium: 78 mg

Blueberry lemon breakfast quinoa

Servings: 2

Preparation time 5 m

Cooking time: *30 m*

ingredients

1 c quinoa

2 c nonfat milk

1 pinch salt

3 tbsps. Maple syrup

1/2 lemon, zested

1 c blueberries

2 tsps. Flax seed

Directions

Using a fine strainer, rinse quinoa with cold water until water isn't frothy anymore and runs clear. This step will remove bitterness from the quinoa.

Over medium heat, pour milk in a saucepan. Heat for 2 to 3 minutes until warm. Add salt and quinoa and then stir. Switch to medium-low heat to simmer for around 20 minutes until the quinoa absorbs most of the milk. Remove from heat and mix in lemon zest and maple syrup and lemon zest. Fold blueberries carefully into the mixture.

Place the quinoa mixture into two bowls. Top each quinoa with a tsp. Of flax seed. Serve.

Nutrition:

Calories: 538

Total fat: 7.3 g

Carbohydrates: 98.7g

Protein: 21.5 g

Cholesterol: 5 mg

Sodium: 112 mg

Blueberry oatmeal

Servings: 2

Preparation time 10 m

Cooking time: *15 m*

ingredients

1 1/3 c water

1 pinch salt

2/3 c quick oats

1 tbsp. Crushed flax seed

1 tbsp. Brown sugar

1 tsp. Ground cinnamon

1 tsp. Vanilla extract

1/2 c milk (optional)

1/4 c fresh blueberries, or more to taste

Directions

In a saucepan, bring salted water to a boil. Stir in oats and cook for 2 to 3 minutes until almost tender. Mix in cinnamon, flax, vanilla extract, and brown sugar. Cook for an additional 2-3 minutes until the liquid is boiled off, the right consistency is achieved, and the oats become tender. Add blueberries and milk then stir.

Nutrition:

Calories: 210

Total fat: 5.6 g

Carbohydrates: 33.3g

Protein: 6.9 g

Cholesterol: 5 mg

Sodium: 36 mg

Bramboracky (Czech savory potato pancakes)

Servings: 3

preparation time 30 m

Cooking time: 1 h

ingredients

4 large potatoes

3 cloves garlic, crushed

Salt and black pepper to taste

1 pinch dried marjoram (optional)

2 tsps. Caraway seeds (optional)

2 eggs

1 tbsp. Milk

3 tbsps. All-purpose flour

Oil for frying

Directions

Peel the potatoes and grate them coarsely. Squeeze out as much liquid as possible. Place the shredded potatoes into a mixing bowl and combine with these ingredients: marjoram, crushed garlic, caraway seeds, pepper, and salt.

Beat the milk and eggs. Then stir the egg mixture into the potatoes. Stir in the flour slowly until a thick batter that can still be poured is formed.

Over medium-high heat, pour oil a quarter-inch deep in a skillet. Use a spoon to transfer a quarter c of batter into the hot oil. Flatten the batter a little. Fry for approximately 3 minutes per side until the pancake turns golden brown. Drain each pancake on paper towels. Adjust the seasoning if needed. Repeat the step until all the remaining batter is used.

Nutrition:

Calories: 527

Total fat: 11.1 g

Carbohydrates: 94.3g

Protein: 15.1 g

Cholesterol: 110 mg

Sodium: 74 mg

Broiled grapefruit

Servings: 8

preparation time 15 m

Cooking time: *18 m*

ingredients

4 grapefruit

1 tbsp. Ground cinnamon

1 tbsp. White sugar

4 tsps. Butter

Directions

Preheat the broiler of your oven.

Slice the grapefruits in half. Remove the sections in the halves using a small serrated knife. Transfer the juice and sections using a spoon into a bowl. Scrape out all the remaining pulp and thick skins. Return the sections to the grapefruit halves using a spoon. Do it one grapefruit half at a time.

Sprinkle cinnamon and sugar on each half. Dot the grapefruit halves with butter and then put them on a cookie sheet.

Broil the grapefruit until the sugar begins to caramelize and the butter melts, for 3-5 minutes.

Nutrition:

Calories: 86

Total fat: 2 g

Carbohydrates: 17.3g

Protein: 1.1 g

Cholesterol: 5 mg

Sodium: 14 mg <

Brown rice breakfast porridge

Servings: 2

Preparation time 5 m

Cooking time: *30 m*

ingredients

1 c cooked brown rice

1 c low-fat milk

2 tbsps. Dried blueberries

1 dash cinnamon

1 tbsp. Honey

1 egg

1/4 tsp. Vanilla extract

1 tbsp. Butter

Directions

In a small saucepan, mix together the blueberries, honey, cooked brown rice, cinnamon, and milk. Let the mixture boil. Adjust the heat to low to simmer for 20 minutes.

In a small bowl, beat the egg and whisk in around six tbsps. Of the hot rice, one tablespoonful at a time. Mix the egg and rice together and then stir in butter and vanilla. Cooking over low heat until the mixture becomes thick, for a minute or two.

Nutrition:

Calories: 318

Total fat: 11.6 g

Carbohydrates: 44.7g

Protein: 9.9 g

Cholesterol: 118 mg

Sodium: 130 mg

Caprese on a stick

Servings: 8

preparation time 15 m

Cooking time: *15 m*

ingredients

1-pint cherry tomatoes, halved

Salt and pepper to taste

Directions

Insert a halved tomato, a small basil leaf, and a ball of mozzarella cheese onto each toothpick. Keep doing it until you've used up all ingredients. Drizzle olive oil but avoid the end of the toothpick. Sprinkle with pepper and salt to taste. Serve right away. Nutrition:

Calories: 215

Total fat: 17.4 g

Carbohydrates: 3g <

Protein: 10.5 g

Cholesterol: 45 mg

Sodium: 133 mg

Carrot cake oatmeal

Servings: 6

Preparation time 15 m

Cooking time: *55 m*

ingredients

4 c water

1 c steel-cut oats

1 apple - peeled, cored, and chopped

1/2 c shredded carrot

1/2 c raisins

1 tsp. Ground cinnamon

1/2 tsp. Ground nutmeg

1/2 tsp. Ground ginger

1 pinch salt

1 tbsp. Butter

3/4 c chopped pecans

1 tbsp. Brown sugar

1/2 c plain yogurt

Directions

In a big and heavy saucepan, pour water and bring it to a boil. Add the oats and stir. Lower the heat and simmer for around 10 minutes until the oats start to become thick. Place the nutmeg, apple, salt, cinnamon, raisins, ginger, and carrot. Mix them all in. Simmer for another 20 minutes until the oats are tender. Meanwhile, place a skillet over medium-low heat. Melt butter and toast the pecans for 2-5 minutes until they turn slightly brown and smell good. Sprinkle with brown sugar. Mix until the sugar has coated the nuts and melted. Serve the oatmeal in several bowls. Top each serving with a dollop of yogurt and around two tbsps. Of the mixture.

Nutrition:

Calories: 287

Total fat: 13.9 g

Carbohydrates: 37.7g

Protein: 6.2 g

Cholesterol: 6 mg

Sodium: 67 mg

Cinnamon stove top granola

Servings: 12

preparation time 10 m

Cooking time: *2 h 20 m*

ingredients

1 1/4 tbsps. Olive oil

5 c rolled oats

1 tbsp. Ground cinnamon

1/3 c butter

1/4 c honey

1 tbsp. Molasses

1/2 c packed brown sugar

1/2 c blanched slivered almonds (optional)

1/2 c dried cherries (optional)

Directions

In a big stockpot, heat the olive oil over medium heat and add the cinnamon and oats. Cook while stirring continuously for 3-4 minutes until the oats are toasted lightly. Transfer to a big baking sheet. Melt butter in the stockpot and mix in the brown sugar, honey, and molasses. Bring to a simmer and place the oats back to the pot. Keep cooking and stirring until hot and coated.

Remove the stockpot from heat. Add the cherries and almonds. Stir and transfer to a big cookie sheet. Let the mixture cool and harden. Store the granola at room temperature in an airtight container.

Nutrition:

Calories: 295

Total fat: 11 g

Carbohydrates: 44.6g

Protein: 5.8 g

Cholesterol: 14 mg

Sodium: 43 mg

Classic hash browns

Servings: 2

Preparation time 10 m

Cooking time: *20 m*

ingredients

2 russet potatoes, peeled

3 tbsps. Clarified butter

Salt and ground black pepper to taste

1 pinch cayenne pepper, or to taste

1 pinch paprika, or to taste

Directions

Fill a big bowl with cold water and shred potatoes into it. Stir until the water is cloudy. Drain and fill the bowl again with fresh cold water. Dissolve extra starch by stirring. Drain potatoes thoroughly and pat them dry using paper towels. Squeeze out excess moisture from the potatoes.

In a big nonstick pan, heat clarified butter over medium heat. Sprinkle shredded potatoes, paprika, salt, cayenne pepper, and black pepper.

Cook for around 5 minutes until a brown crust forms on the bottom of the pan. Keep on cooking and stirring for another 5 minutes until potatoes are fully browned.

Nutrition:

Calories: 334

Total fat: 19.4 g

Carbohydrates: 37.5g

Protein: 4.4 g

Cholesterol: 49 mg

Sodium: 13 mg <

Coconut granola

Servings: *24*

Preparation time *20 m*

Cooking time: *36 m*

ingredients

8 c quick-cooking oats

1 c oat bran

1 c unsweetened flaked coconut

3/4 c chopped almonds

1/2 c coconut milk

1/2 c dried cranberries

Directions

Set an oven to 350*0* Fahrenheit (175*0* Celsius) to preheat. Combine the coconut, oats, almonds, and oat bran in a big bowl. Spread the mixture evenly onto two big baking sheets.

Bake the mixture for 7 or 8 minutes until it's toasted lightly. Remove from oven and let it cool for a little while. Place it back in the big bowl.

As the oats are toasting, mix together these ingredients in a saucepan: malt syrup, coconut milk, vegetable oil, honey, and coconut oil. Over medium heat, bring to a boil while stirring. Keep boiling for 2 minutes and remove from heat. Add the vanilla and stir. In the bowl, pour the syrup over the granola. Then stir to fully coat the dry ingredients with syrup. Spread evenly onto two baking sheets.

Place the baking sheets in the oven and bake until toasted and fragrant or for 8 minutes. Allow the granola to cool before stirring in the dried cranberries. Store the granola at room temperature in an airtight container.

Nutrition:

Calories: 267

Total fat: 12.3 g

Carbohydrates: 36.4g

Protein: 6.1 g

Cholesterol: 0 mg

Sodium: 7 mg <

Cranberry-orange spiced oatmeal

Servings: 1

preparation time 5 m

Cooking time: 7 m

ingredients

3/4 c old-fashioned rolled oats

1/2 tsp. Ground cinnamon, or to taste

1/4 c dried cranberries

1/2 c frozen blueberries

1/4 tsp. Ground turmeric (optional)

1 pinch ground ginger (optional)

1 c water

1/4 c orange juice, or as needed

Directions

In a microwave-safe bowl, put the cranberries, cinnamon, blueberries, and rolled oats. You can throw in turmeric and ginger if you like. Mix in the water and place in the microwave. Cook on high setting for around 2 minutes until the oatmeal has absorbed the water. Pour in orange juice until you've reached the right consistency.

Nutrition:

Calories: 398

Total fat: 4.5 g

Carbohydrates: 84.8g

Protein: 9.1 g

Cholesterol: 0 mg

Sodium: 13 mg <

Creamy apple cinnamon raisin oatmeal

Servings: 2

Preparation time 5 m

Cooking time: *15 m*

ingredients

2 c water

2 tsps. Brown sugar

1 tsp. Ground cinnamon

2 tbsps. Maple syrup

1 c uncooked rolled oats

2 tbsps. Raisins

1 apple - peeled, cored and cubed

Directions

Mix together cinnamon, water, syrup, and brown sugar in a medium-sized saucepan. Bring to a boil.

Lower the heat. Put the oats and cook until they absorb all water, for approximately 5 minutes. Remove the pan from heat. Before serving, mix in raisins and apples.

Nutrition:

Calories: 293

Total fat: 2.9 g

Carbohydrates: 64g

Protein: 5.9 g

Cholesterol: 0 mg

Sodium: 7 mg <

Crunchy pumpkin pie granola

Servings: *10*

Preparation time 15 m

Cooking time: *1 h 45 m*

ingredients

1/3 c brown sugar

1 tbsp. Pumpkin pie spice

3 1/2 c rolled oats

1/2 c sliced almonds

1/2 c chopped pecans

2/3 c applesauce

1/2 c honey

1 tbsp. Vanilla extract

1/2 c raisins

1/2 c dried cranberries

Directions

Turn your oven to 250o Fahrenheit (120o Celsius) to preheat. Spray two baking sheets with nonstick cooking spray.

In a big bowl, mix together rolled oats, pecans, brown sugar, almonds, and pumpkin pie spice. Get another big bowl and combine the honey, vanilla, and applesauce. Mix the oat mixture into the applesauce mixture. Stir until the granola starts to form clusters. Spread the granola evenly using a spoon onto prepared baking sheets.

Place the baking sheets in the oven. Bake for around an hour, stirring per 20 minutes, until the granola becomes crispy and browned lightly.

Cool the granola at room temperature. Mix in cranberries and raisins and cranberries before storing the granola in an airtight container.

Nutrition:

Calories: 312

Total fat: 8.6 g

Carbohydrates: 55.9g

Protein: 5.6 g

Cholesterol: 0 mg

Sodium: 6 mg <

Dad's Kentucky home fries

Servings: 4

Preparation time 10 m

Cooking time: *25 m*

ingredients

2 tbsps. Bacon drippings

4 large potatoes, peeled and sliced

1/2 Vidalia onion, chopped

Salt and pepper to taste

Directions

In a big skillet, heat the bacon drippings over medium heat. Stir in the onion and potatoes. Cook while stirring from time to time for around 15 minutes, until potatoes become golden brown and tender. Add pepper and salt to taste. Serve.

Nutrition:

Calories: 352

Total fat: 7.3 g

Carbohydrates: 65.7g

Protein: 7.6 g

Cholesterol: 7 mg

Sodium: 33 mg

Chapter 20: Soups, stews and sauces

Crockpot Cranberry Applesauce Recipe

Preparation time: 15minutes

Cooking time: 4-6 hours

Serves 8

Ingredients:

10 apples such as golden delicious, peeled and roughly chopped

12oz cranberries, rinsed and drained

Instructions:

1. Place fruit in a 5-quart crockpot and mix well.

2. Cover crockpot and cook on LOW for 4 - 6 hours or until everything is cooked and the fruit has dissolved into a sauce.

3. You can add sweetener if desired or use a blender if you prefer a less chunky sauce.

Nutrition: Calories 113, Fat 0g, Carbs 28g, Protein 0g, Fiber 0g, Potassium 185mg, Sodium 1mg

Marinara Sauce

Preparation time: 15 minutes

Cooking time: 3-4 hours

Serves 12

Ingredients:

10 garlic cloves, minced

1 14oz can no-added sodium diced tomatoes

1 14oz can no-added sodium crushed tomatoes

2 tbsp no-added sodium tomato paste

2 tbsp fresh basil, minced

1 tbsp onion powder

1 tbsp Italian seasoning

2 tsp balsamic vinegar

Directions

1. Place all ingredients into a 3 or 4-quart slow cooker and mix well.

2. Cover and cook on LOW for around 3-4 hours.

3. Serve with pasta, chicken, meat, and fish. The sauce keeps well for up to 2 weeks in a refrigerator and you can also freeze the sauce.

Nutrition: Calories 292, Fat 0g, Carbs 6g, Protein 1g, Fiber 1g, Potassium 219mg, Sodium 116mg

Low Sodium Chicken Broth

Preparation time: 5 minutes

Cooking time: 4 hours

Serves 10

Ingredients:

1 medium carrot, cut into 1-inch pieces

1 stalk celery, cut into 1-inch pieces

1 small onion, cut into 1-inch pieces

4lb skinless chicken leg quarters

6 sprigs fresh parsley

2 sprigs fresh thyme

1 bay leaf

1 garlic clove, minced

20 whole peppercorns

9 cup water

Directions

1. Place all ingredients in a 6-quart slow cooker.

2. Cover and cook on HIGH for 4 hours.

3. Leave to cool and then strain well.

4. Use the cooked chicken for other dishes. The strained broth is flavorsome and the perfect base for countless dishes yet is virtually calorie and sodium-free. The broth can be refrigerated or frozen.

Nutrition: Calories 34, Fat <1g, Carbs 3g, Protein 4g, Fiber 0g, Potassium 145mg, Sodium 39mg

Blueberry Butter

Preparation time: 15 minutes

Cooking time: 5-6 hours

Serves 16

Ingredients:

5 cup blueberries, pureed

1 cup sugar

2 tsp ground cinnamon

1 medium lemon, zested and juiced

Directions

1. Place all ingredients in a 6-quart slow cooker and mix well.

2. Cover and cook on LOW for 1 hour.

3. Use a heat-safe kitchen utensil such as a wooden spoon to prop the lid slightly open while you continue to cook for a further 4-5 hours, stirring every hour.

4. The blueberry butter is ready when it has thickened and coats the back of a spoon.

5. The sauce can be stored in a refrigerator for up to 2 weeks in an airtight container and can also be frozen.

. *Nutrition:* Calories 102, Fat 0g, Carbs 27g, Protein 1g, Fiber 2g, Potassium 64mg, Sodium 1mg

Low Sodium Beef Broth

Preparation time: 20 minutes

Cooking time: 8 hours

Serves 10

Ingredients:

3lb soup bones

1lb beef shank

4 large carrots, peeled and cut into 1-inch chunks

2 medium onions, peeled and chopped

2 tbsp olive oil

2 bay leaves

5 garlic cloves, peeled and crushed

5 peppercorns

8 cup water

Directions

1. Preheat oven to 400°F.

2. Place the bones, beef shank, and vegetables in a large roasting pan drizzled with the oil and roast for 2 hours until brown.

3. Place the beef, bones, and vegetables into a 5 or a 6-quart slow cooker along with the bay, garlic, and peppercorns.

4. Use 1 cup of water to scrape up the meat juices and add to the slow cooker with the remaining water.

5. Cover and cook on LOW for 8 hours.

6. Chill the broth overnight, then strain well to remove all the solidified fat.

7. The strained broth is flavorsome and the perfect base for countless dishes yet is virtually calorie and sodium-free. The broth can be refrigerated or frozen.

Nutrition: Calories 20, Fat <1g, Carbs 0g, Protein 3g, Fiber 0g, Potassium 206mg, Sodium 20mg

Coney Dog Sauce

Preparation time: 20 minutes

Cooking time: 4 hours

Serves 8

Ingredients:

1lb lean ground beef

2 cup low-sodium tomato sauce

½ cup water

1½ tbsp low-sodium Worcestershire sauce

¼ cup onion, finely chopped

1 tbsp ground mustard

½ tsp garlic powder

½ tsp freshly ground black pepper

½ tsp chili powder

¼ tsp cayenne pepper

Directions

1. Brown the ground beef in a large heavy-based frying pan.

2. Add the cooked ground beef along with all other ingredients to a 4 to 6-quart slow cooker.

3. Cover and cook on LOW for 4 hours.

4. Serve as a topping with low-sodium hot dogs.

Nutrition: Calories 112, Fat 4g, Carbs 5g, Protein 12g, Fiber 1g, Potassium 210mg, Sodium 83mg

Cranberry Sauce

Preparation time: 10 minutes

Cooking time: 5-6 hours

Serves 10

Ingredients:

12oz cranberries

½ cup orange juice

1 large cinnamon stick

½ cup honey

Directions

1. Place all the ingredients into a 2 or a 3-quart slow cooker and mix well.

2. Cook for 5-6 hours on LOW, or until the berries are soft and have dissolved down.

3. Remove the lid and continue to cook for 1-2 hours on HIGH until the sauce has thickened.

4. The sauce can be stored in a refrigerator for up to 2 weeks in an airtight container and can also be frozen.

Nutrition: Calories 73, Fat 0g, Carbs 19g, Protein 0g, Fiber 2g, Potassium 65mg, Sodium 1mg

Creamy Potato Soup

Preparation time:15 minutes

Cooking time: 4 hours

Serves 8

Ingredients:

Soup Ingredients

5 cup potatoes, peeled and diced

2 cup cauliflower, diced

2/3 cup celery, diced

1 cup onion, diced

6–8 cloves garlic, minced

4 cup sodium-free chicken broth (see recipe)

½ tsp dried thyme

¼ tsp dried cilantro

Roux Ingredients

1 tbsp butter

¼ cup all-purpose flour

1 1/3 cup skim milk

¼ tsp black pepper

½ tsp low sodium salt

Directions

1. Place all soup ingredients in a 5 to 6-quart slow cooker.

2. Cook on HIGH for 4 hours.

3. Puree the soup with a blender.

4. Make a roux by melting the butter and adding the flour in a small heavy-based pan.

5. Cook for 3 to 4 minutes.

6. Gradually add the milk until you have a thickened sauce.

7. Season the sauce, then stir into the soup and heat through before serving.

Nutrition: Calories 396, Fat 18g, Cholesterol 61mg, Carbs 7g, Protein 20g, Fiber 2g, Potassium 1222mg, Sodium 420mg

Creamy Cauliflower & Butternut Squash Soup

Preparation time: 5 minutes

Cooking time: 2 hours

Serves 6

Ingredients:

1 onion, diced

1-2 tsp oil for sautéing

2-3 cloves garlic, minced

7 cup cauliflower florets

2 cup butternut squash, cubed

2 cup sodium-free vegetable or chicken broth (see recipe)

1 tsp paprika

1 tsp dried thyme

½ tsp red pepper flakes

¼ tsp low sodium salt

½ cup half and half

Directions

1. Sauté onion and garlic in a heavy-based skillet.

2. Place in a 5 to 6-quart with all other ingredients except the half and half.

3. Cook on HIGH for 4 hours.

4. Puree the soup in a blender.

5. Stir in the half and half, heat through and serve.

Nutrition: Calories 100, Fat 2g, Carbs 16g, Protein 3g, Fiber 6g, Potassium 553mg, Sodium 345mg

Crock Pot Turkey & Sweet Potato Chipotle Chili

Preparation time:15 minutes

Cooking time: 4 hours

Serves 8

Ingredients:

4 cup sweet potatoes, peeled and chopped

2– 2 ½ cup broth

1lb lean ground turkey

14 oz diced low-sodium canned tomatoes

1 cup onion, chopped

2 –3 cup cauliflower, finely chopped

1 tsp garlic, minced

2 chipotles, chopped

1 tsp cumin

½ tsp paprika

½ tsp chili powder

¼ tsp black pepper

½ tsp low-sodium salt

½ cup bell peppers, chopped

Directions

1. Par-cook the potatoes until tender and place in a 4 to 6-quart slow cooker.

2. Brown meat in a skillet, then add to slow cooker.

3. Add all remaining ingredients to slow cooker and mix well.

4. Cover and cook on HIGH for 3-4 hrs.

5. Check the seasoning and garnish with fresh cilantro and finely chopped jalapenos.

Nutrition: Calories 311, Fat 12g, Carbs 21g, Protein 19g, Fiber 2g, Potassium 565mg, Sodium 211mg

Beef & Barley Stew

Preparation time: 5 minutes

Cooking time: 6-8 hours

Serves 6

Ingredients:

1 cup pearl barley, uncooked

1lb lean beef stew meat, cut into 1-inch cubes

2 tbsp all-purpose white flour

¼ tsp black pepper

½ tsp low-sodium salt

2 tbsp canola oil

½ cup onion

1 large stalk celery, diced

1 garlic clove, minced

2 medium carrots, diced

2 bay leaves

2 quarts water

1 tsp salt-free Mrs. Dash® onion herb seasoning

Directions

1. Soak barley in 2 cups of water for 1 hour. Place in a 4-quart slow cooker.

2. Dust the meat in the black pepper and flour.

3. Heat the oil in a skillet and brown the meat. Add to the slow cooker.

4. Sauté the vegetables and garlic for a few minutes and add to the slow cooker.

5. Add the water and seasoning.

6. Cover and cook on LOW for 6-8 hours.

Nutrition: Calories 246, Fat 8g, Carbs 21g, Protein 22g, Fiber 6g, Potassium 369mg, Sodium 150mg

Healthy Crockpot White Chicken Chili

Preparation time: 30minutes

Cooking time: 6-8 hours

Serves 8

Ingredients:

2-3 large boneless skinless chicken breasts

2 15.50z cans of reduced-sodium great northern beans, drained and rinsed

1 150z of sweet golden corn, drained well and rinsed

1 4.50z can green chilies, chopped

4 cup chicken broth (see recipe)

1 medium sweet yellow onion, chopped

3 garlic cloves, minced

1 lime, juiced

1 tsp cumin

½ tsp onion powder

½ tsp garlic powder

1 ½ tsp chili powder

¼ tsp cayenne pepper

1 tsp black pepper

1 tsp paprika

Directions

Add chicken broth and squeeze the juice of one lime over the mixture.

Cook on LOW for 6 to 8 hours.

Before removing from the slow cooker, shred the chicken with forks.

Nutrition: Calories 300, Fat 2g, Carbs 30g, Protein 32g, Fiber 6g, Potassium 549mg, Sodium 324mg

Green Chili Stew

Preparation time: 20 minutes

Cooking time: 10 hours

Serves 6

Ingredients:

½ cup all-purpose flour

1 tbsp garlic powder

1 tsp black pepper

1lb lean boneless pork chops, cut into 1-inch cubes

1 tbsp olive oil

1 8oz can of green chili peppers, drained well and chopped

1 garlic clove, minced

2 cup chicken broth (see recipe)

6 flour tortillas, burrito size

¾ cup iceberg lettuce, shredded

¼ cup cilantro, finely chopped

6 tbsp sour cream

Directions

1. Place the flour, garlic powder, and black pepper into a Ziploc bag.

2. Add the pork and coat well.

3. Heat the oil in a skillet and brown the pork.

4. Add the pork to a 4-quart slow cooker along with the broth, peppers, and garlic.

5. Cover and cook for 10 hours on LOW.

6. Place lettuce on a tortilla, top with stew and roll up burrito style.

7. Top with sour cream and cilantro.

Nutrition: Calories 420, Fat 16g, Carbs 44g, Protein 25g, Fiber 3g, Potassium 454mg, Sodium 352mg

Turkey, Wild Rice, and Mushroom Soup

Preparation time: 15 minutes

Cooking time: 2-3 hours

Serves 6

Ingredients:

½ cup onion, chopped

½ cup red bell pepper, chopped

½ cup carrots, chopped

2 garlic cloves, minced

2 cup cooked turkey, shredded

5 cup chicken broth (see recipe)

½ cup quick-cooking wild rice, uncooked

1 tbsp olive oil

1 cup mushrooms, sliced

2 bay leaves

¼ tsp Mrs. Dash® Original salt-free herb seasoning blend

1 tsp dried thyme

½ tsp low sodium salt

¼ tsp black pepper

Directions

1. Cook rice in a saucepan with 1-2 cups of broth. Set aside.

2. Heat oil in a skillet and sauté the onion, bell pepper, carrots, and garlic until soft. Add to a 4 to 6-quart slow cooker.

3. Add remaining ingredients to the slow cooker except for the rice and mushrooms.

4. Cover and cook for 2-3 hours on LOW.

5. Add the mushrooms and rice and cook for a further 15 minutes.

6. Remove the bay leaves and serve.

Nutrition: Calories 210, Fat 2g, Carbs 15g, Protein 23g, Fiber 2g, Potassium 380mg, Sodium 115mg

Veggie Soup

Preparation time: 20 minutes

Cooking time: 6 hours

Serves 6

Ingredients:

1 14oz no salt added diced tomatoes

1 large onion, diced

4 garlic cloves, minced

2 large carrots, diced

2 celery stalks, diced

1 medium parsnip, diced

1 large red bell pepper, diced

6 cup low sodium vegetable or chicken broth (see recipe)

3 cup cabbage, chopped

½ tsp low sodium salt

½ tsp black pepper

1 large sweet potato, peeled and diced

Directions

1. Place all ingredients in a slow cooker.

2. Cook for 4-6 hours on HIGH.

3. Serve the soup chunky or puree if desired.

Nutrition: Calories 135, Fat 1g, Carbs 30g, Protein 4g, Fiber 7g, Potassium 880mg, Sodium 250mg

Goldy's Special Salad

Servings: 4

preparation time *20 m*

cooking time: *20 m*

ingredients

2 tbsps. Extra virgin olive oil

1/2 c white wine vinegar

1/2 tsp. Ground black pepper

1 pinch white sugar

Directions

Mix together the tomato, mushrooms, spinach, onion, mango, and avocado in a big salad bowl.

In a jar, combine the pepper, oil, sugar, and vinegar. Seal the jar and shake it well. Pour the dressing over the salad. Toss before serving.

Nutrition:

Calories: 216

Total fat: 14.8 g

Carbohydrates: 20.4g

Protein: 5.5 g

Cholesterol: 0 mg

Sodium: 68 mg

Grandma's sweet slaw

Servings: 8

preparation time 15 m

cooking time: *15 m*

ingredients

1/2 c white sugar

1/2 c mayonnaise

3 medium carrots, shredded

1 medium head cabbage, cored and shredded

Directions

Combine the mayonnaise and sugar in a big bowl. Mix in the cabbage and carrots. Toss to coat. Chill in the fridge before serving.

Nutrition:

Calories: 185

Total fat: 11.1 g

Carbohydrates: 21.7g

Protein: 1.8 g

Cholesterol: 5 mg

Sodium: 114 mg

Green bean and potato salad

Servings: *10*

Preparation time 15 m

cooking time: *45 m*

ingredients

1 1/2 pounds red potatoes

3/4-pound fresh green beans, trimmed and snapped

1/4 c chopped fresh basil

1 small red onion, chopped

Salt and pepper to taste

1/4 c balsamic vinegar

2 tbsps. Dijon mustard

2 tbsps. Fresh lemon juice

1 clove garlic, minced

1 dash Worcestershire sauce

1/2 c extra virgin olive oil

Directions

In a big pot, put the potatoes and pour in water until it reaches a level of 1 inch. Bring to a boil. Cook the potatoes until they're tender for around 15 minutes. After the first 10 minutes, drop the green beans into the pot to steam. Drain the potatoes and green beans. Allow them to cool. Cut potatoes into four equal pieces. Place the potato wedges and green beans in a big bowl. Season with salt, basil, pepper, and red onion. Toss and set aside.

Prepare the dressing in a medium-sized bowl. Whisk together the lemon juice, balsamic vinegar, olive oil, garlic, Worcestershire sauce, and mustard. Pour the mixture over the salad. Stir to coat. Add more pepper and salt if you want.

Nutrition:

Calories: 176

Total fat: 11.3 g

Carbohydrates: 17.4g

Protein: 1.9 g

Cholesterol: 0 mg

Sodium: 82 mg

Grilled orange vinaigrette chicken salad

Servings: 6

Preparation time 15 m

cooking time: *35 m*

ingredients

1/2 c orange juice

1/2 c white wine vinegar

1/4 c olive oil

4 tbsps. Salt-free garlic and herb seasoning blend

1 1/2 tbsps. White sugar

1-pound skinless, boneless chicken breast halves

1 head romaine lettuce-rinsed, dried and chopped

1 (11 ounce) can mandarin oranges, drained

1 c chopped fresh broccoli

1 c chopped baby carrots

Directions

Set a grill on medium-high heat to preheat.

Whisk together the olive oil, orange juice, sugar, seasoning blend, and vinegar in a bowl. Reserve around half a c of the mixture for basting later.

Oil the grate of the grill lightly. Cook the chicken breast on the preheated grill until juices of the meat run clear or for 6-8 minutes per side. While grilling, baste constantly with half a c of the reserved sauce. Let the grilled chicken cool. Then cut the meat into strips. Discard the sauce.

Toss together the broccoli, lettuce, carrots, and oranges in a big bowl. Put the chicken strips on top of the salad. Drizzle with the remaining sauce. Serve.

Nutrition:

Calories: 239

Total fat: 11.1 g

Carbohydrates: 17.5g

Protein: 17.2 g

Cholesterol: 43 mg

Sodium: 69 mg

Grilled romaine salad

Servings: 8

preparation time 30 m

cooking time: *3 h 10 m*

ingredients

1/2 c olive oil

3 tbsps. White sugar

1 tsp. Dried rosemary

1 tsp. Dried thyme

1/4 tsp. Salt

1/4 tsp. Ground black pepper

Directions

Chop the shallots finely in a food processor or blender. Add the brown sugar and vinegar to the chopped shallots. Process the ingredients until the mixture is smooth. Pour in 1.75 c of oil gradually, processing constantly until the mixture becomes thick.

Put a grill on high heat to preheat. Brush romaine hearts with a tbsp. Of olive oil. Add pepper and salt.

Grill the romaine hearts, turning many times, for 5-10 minutes. They should be charred slightly yet not heated throughout. Transfer grilled romaine hearts to salad plates. Place the tomatoes around them. Then drizzle with the dressing.

Nutrition:

Calories: 622

Total fat: 62.8 g

Carbohydrates: 16.6g

Protein: 1.5 g

Cholesterol: 0 mg

Sodium: 87 mg

Hawaiian Cole slaw

Servings: *16*

Preparation time 10 m

cooking time: *10 m*

ingredients

1 (8.5 ounce) package coleslaw mix

1 (15 ounce) can crushed pineapple, drained

1/2 c finely chopped onion

1/2 c mayonnaise

1/4 c apple cider vinegar

2 tbsps. Brown sugar

1 tsp. Dried cilantro

1/2 tsp. Salt

1/4 tsp. Ground black pepper

Directions

In a bowl, combine the pineapple, coleslaw mix, and onion.

Get another bowl to prepare the dressing. Whisk together the cilantro, pepper, mayonnaise, salt, vinegar, and brown sugar until the mixture becomes smooth. Pour the dressing over the coleslaw mixture. Toss to coat and chill in the fridge.

Nutrition:

Calories: 86

Total fat: 5.9 g

Carbohydrates: 8.4g

Protein: 0.4 g <

Cholesterol: 4 mg

Sodium: 116 mg

Herb watermelon feta salad

Servings: 12

preparation time *20 m*

cooking time: *20 m*

ingredients

1 (4 ounce) package crumbled feta cheese

3 tbsps. Olive oil

2 tbsps. Balsamic vinegar, or more to taste

Salt and ground black pepper to taste

Directions

In a big bow, slowly toss together the lime juice, black pepper, watermelon, salt, onion, balsamic vinegar, basil, olive oil, cilantro, feta cheese, and mint. Nutrition:

Calories: 177

Total fat: 6 g

Carbohydrates: 31.1g

Protein: 4 g

Cholesterol: 8 mg

Sodium: 112 mg

Hot fruit salad

Servings: 12

preparation time 10 m

cooking time: *1 h 40 m*

ingredients

1 (20 ounce) jar chunky applesauce

1 (21 ounce) can cherry pie filling

1 (15 ounce) can sliced peaches, drained

1 (11 ounce) can mandarin orange segments, drained

1 (8 ounce) can pineapple chunks

1/2 c brown sugar

1 tsp. Ground cinnamon

Directions

In a slow cooker, put the peaches, cinnamon, applesauce, brown sugar, cherry pie filling, pineapple, and mandarin oranges. Cover the slow cooker. Cook for 1.5 hours on low.

Nutrition:

Calories: 148

Total fat: 0.1 g <

Carbohydrates: 37.7g

Protein: 0.7 g

Cholesterol: 0 mg

Sodium: 15 mg <

Chapter 21: Cucumber and beans

Cool summer cucumber and tomato toss

Servings: 4

preparation time 15 m

cooking time: *15 m*

ingredients

1 large cucumber, peeled and sliced

2 ripe fresh tomatoes, chopped

2 tbsps. Balsamic vinegar

2 tbsps. Olive oil

Salt and pepper to taste

Directions

In a bowl, put the tomatoes and cucumber and pour in the balsamic vinegar and olive oil. Add pepper and salt. Coat everything by gently tossing. Chill in the fridge before serving the salad.

Nutrition:

Calories: 84

Total fat: 7 g

Carbohydrates: 5.3g

Protein: 1 g

Cholesterol: 0 mg

Sodium: 103 mg

Mizeria (polish cucumber salad)

Servings: 12

preparation time 10 m

cooking time: *45 m*

ingredients

1-pound small cucumbers, peeled and thinly sliced

Salt to taste

1 bunch dill, chopped

2 1/2 tbsps. Sour cream

1 tsp. Lemon juice

Directions

In a bowl, place the cucumbers and sprinkle with salt. Leave for 5 minutes until soft. Squeeze out excess moisture. Add dill to the salted cucumbers.

Get another bowl and combine the lemon juice, sour cream, and sugar. Toss the dressing with the cucumbers to coat. Add black pepper. Chill in the refrigerator for half an hour or longer.

Nutrition:

Calories: 13<

Total fat: 0.7 g

Carbohydrates: 1.4g <

Protein: 0.4 g <

Cholesterol: 1 mg <

Sodium: 36 mg

Cranberry lentil and quinoa salad

Servings: 12

preparation time 15 m

cooking time: *2 h* INGREDIENTS

Salad:

1 c dried lentils

2 bay leaves, divided (optional)

Water to cover

2 c water

1 c quinoa

Dressing:

3 tbsps. Lemon juice

1 tsp. Honey

1 tbsp. White wine vinegar

1/4 tsp. Salt

3 tbsps. Olive oil

Ground black pepper to taste

1/2 c coarsely chopped walnuts, toasted

1/2 c dried cranberries, or to taste

1/2 c crumbled feta cheese

1 small green onion, finely chopped

Directions

In a saucepan, put a bay leaf and the lentils. Cover them with enough water. Bring to a boil. Over medium-low heat, simmer the lentils for around half an hour until they're tender. Drain the lentils and remove the bay leaf. Rinse the lentils with cold water. When the lentils are cool, place them in a big bowl.

In a saucepan, put the quinoa, two c of water, quinoa, and remaining bay leaf. Bring to a boil and adjust to medium-low heat. With the pan covered, simmer the quinoa for 15-20 minutes until it becomes tender and has absorbed the water. Rinse with cold water and remove the bay leaf. When the cooked quinoa is cool, mix it with the lentils.

In a microwave-safe bowl, heat the lemon juice in a microwave for half a minute until it gets warm. Dissolve honey into the lemon juice. Pour in the vinegar and add the salt. Whisk in the olive oil and black pepper. Pour the lemon juice mixture into the mixture of quinoa and lentils.

Add the feta cheese, walnuts, green onion, and cranberries to the lentil-and-quinoa salad. Toss the mixture until coated. Chill the salad in the refrigerator for around an hour.

Nutrition:

Calories: 205

Total fat: 8.9 g

Carbohydrates: 24.7g

Protein: 7.8 g

Cholesterol: 6 mg

Sodium: 123 mg

Cranberry Walldorf

Servings: 12

preparation time 15 m

cooking time: *2 h 15 m*

ingredients

1 1/2 c chopped cranberries

1 c chopped red apple

1 c chopped celery

1 c seedless green grapes, halved

1/3 c raisins

1/4 c chopped walnuts

2 tbsps. White sugar

1/4 tsp. Ground cinnamon

1 (8 ounce) container vanilla low-fat yogurt

Directions

Mix together the cranberries, yogurt, apple, cinnamon, celery, sugar, grapes, walnuts, and raisins in a medium-sized bowl. (if you have a food processor, chop the cranberries in its first). Toss the ingredients to evenly coat. Cover the bowl and place it in the fridge. Refrigerate for 2 hours. Stir the cold salad before serving it.

Nutrition:

Calories: 75

Total fat: 2 g

Carbohydrates: 14g

Protein: 1.7 g

Cholesterol: < 1 mg <

Sodium: 22 mg <

Cucumber and yogurt salad

Servings: *7*

Preparation time 15 m

cooking time: *1 h 15 m*

ingredients

3 cucumbers

2 cloves garlic, minced

Salt to taste

2 tbsps. Dried mint

1 c plain yogurt

1 tbsp. Olive oil

Directions

Peel the cucumbers and cut them vertically into four pieces. Remove the seeds. Cut the quartered cucumbers into thin slices and then combine with garlic. In a salad bowl, place the sliced cucumbers in layers. Sprinkle every layer with a bit of salt. Leave the cucumber slices for half an hour.

Firmly press the cucumbers to remove any excess liquid. Crumble the dried mint over cucumber slices.

Beat the yogurt until it's smooth. If you want, you can blend the yogurt in a drizzle of olive oil. Pour the yogurt dressing over the sliced cucumbers. Chill in the fridge.

Nutrition:

Calories: 55

Total fat: 2.6 g

Carbohydrates: 6.1g

Protein: 2.5 g

Cholesterol: 2 mg <

Sodium: 28 mg

Cucumber salad

Servings: 12

preparation time 10 m

cooking time: *2 h 10 m*

ingredients

4 medium cucumbers, peeled and diced

1 tbsp. Dried dill weed

Salt and pepper to taste

Directions

On paper towels, drain the diced cucumbers for a few minutes. Combine the yogurt, dill, garlic, onion, and sour cream in a serving dish. Add the cucumbers to the dressing. Mix gently to coat and season the salad with pepper and salt. For an excellent flavor, chill the cucumber salad in the refrigerator for several hours. Serve cold.

Nutrition:

Calories: 55

Total fat: 2.6 g

Carbohydrates: 6.8g

Protein: 2.1 g

Cholesterol: 8 mg

Sodium: 22 mg <

Cucumber, tomato, and red onion salad

Servings: 6

Preparation time *20 m*

cooking time: *20 m*

ingredients

1/4 c chopped fresh cilantro

Juice of 1 fresh lime

Salt to taste

Directions

In a bowl, combine the tomatoes, red onion, lime juice, cilantro, and cucumbers. Add salt to taste.

Nutrition:

Calories: 41

Total fat: 0.3 g <

Carbohydrates: 9.5g

Protein: 1.7 g

Cholesterol: 0 mg

Sodium: 73 mg

Cucumbers in sour cream

Servings: 12

preparation time 10 m

cooking time: *4 h 10 m*

ingredients

2 cucumbers, thinly sliced

1 (8 ounce) container sour cream

1/4 c distilled white vinegar

1/3 c white sugar

Salt and ground black pepper to taste

Directions

Get a container and put the sliced cucumbers in it. Then cover with cold water. Place the container in the refrigerator. Chill for at least 4 hours up to overnight.

In a mixing bowl, whisk the sugar, sour cream, salt, and vinegar. When the sugar dissolves, drain the cucumbers and squeeze out the excess liquid. Put the cucumbers in the bowl. Mix to coat with the dressing.

Nutrition:

Calories: 69

Total fat: 4 g

Carbohydrates: 8.1g

Protein: 0.9 g

Cholesterol: 8 mg

Sodium: 11 mg <

Garbanzo bean and quinoa salad

Servings: 8

preparation time 15 m

cooking time: *1 h 30 m*

ingredients

1 c quinoa

2 c water

1 (15 ounce) can garbanzo beans, drained

1/2 c dried cranberries

1/2 c golden raisins

1/3 c sliced almonds

1/4 c mint leaves, chopped

3/4 tsp. Ground coriander

1/4 tsp. Ground cumin

1 tbsp. Extra-virgin olive oil

Salt and pepper to taste

Directions

In a saucepan, combine water with quinoa. Bring to a boil over high heat. Adjust to medium-low heat and cover the pan. Simmer the quinoa for 15-20 minutes until it has absorbed the water and has become tender. Transfer to a big bowl and chill in the fridge.

Combine the almonds, olive oil, garbanzo beans, cranberries, cumin, raisins, coriander, and mint. Stir the mixture into the quinoa. Add pepper and salt to taste.

Nutrition:

Calories: 212

Total fat: 5.4 g

Carbohydrates: 36.6g

Protein: 5.8 g

Cholesterol: 0 mg

Sodium: 112 mg

Green bean and potato salad

Servings: *10*

Preparation time 15 m

cooking time: *45 m*

ingredients

1 1/2 pounds red potatoes

3/4-pound fresh green beans, trimmed and snapped

1/4 c chopped fresh basil

1 small red onion, chopped

Salt and pepper to taste

1/4 c balsamic vinegar

2 tbsps. Dijon mustard

2 tbsps. Fresh lemon juice

1 clove garlic, minced

1 dash Worcestershire sauce

1/2 c extra virgin olive oil

Directions

In a big pot, put the potatoes and pour in water until it reaches a level of 1 inch. Bring to a boil. Cook the potatoes until they're tender for around 15 minutes. After the first 10 minutes, drop the green beans into the pot to steam. Drain the potatoes and green beans. Allow them to cool. Cut potatoes into four equal pieces. Place the potato wedges and green beans in a big bowl. Season with salt, basil, pepper, and red onion. Toss and set aside.

Prepare the dressing in a medium-sized bowl. Whisk together the lemon juice, balsamic vinegar, olive oil, garlic, Worcestershire sauce, and mustard. Pour the mixture over the salad. Stir to coat. Add more pepper and salt if you want.

Nutrition:

Calories: 176

Total fat: 11.3 g

Carbohydrates: 17.4g

Protein: 1.9 g

Cholesterol: 0 mg

Sodium: 82 mg

Chapter 22: First course recipes

Spaghetti with Garlic and Basil

Servings: 8

preparation time 15 m

cooking time: *25 m*

ingredients

1 (16 ounce) package uncooked spaghetti

1/4 c extra-virgin olive oil

1/4 c unsalted butter, melted

4 cloves garlic, minced

1 c fresh basil, coarsely chopped

Salt and pepper to taste

1/2 c freshly grated parmesan cheese

Directions

Cook spaghetti in a big pot of boiling salted water until tender yet firm to the bite for 8-10 minutes. Drain.

Toss the pasta with the basil, olive oil, pepper, butter, salt, and garlic in a big bowl. When the mixture is coated evenly, top with parmesan.

Nutrition:

Calories: 336

Total fat: 15.2 g

Carbohydrates: 40.5g

Protein: 8.9 g

Cholesterol: 20 mg

Sodium: 79 mg

Spicy pasta

Servings: 6

Preparation time 10 m

cooking time: *30 m*

ingredients

1 (12 ounce) package rotini pasta

1 tbsp. Vegetable oil

1 clove garlic, crushed

1 tsp. Dried basil

1 tsp. Italian seasoning

1 onion, diced

2 red chile peppers, seeded and chopped

1 (14.5 ounce) can diced tomatoes

3 drops hot pepper sauce

Salt and ground black pepper to taste

Directions

Cook the rotini in a big pot of boiling, lightly salted water until al dente or for 8-10 minutes. Drain the pasta.

In a saucepan, heat oil over medium heat. Sauté garlic, Italian seasoning, and basil for 2-3 minutes. Cook and stir in the chiles and onion. When the onion becomes tender, mix in the hot sauce and tomatoes. Simmer until heated through or for 5 minutes. Toss the sauce with the pasta. Then add pepper and salt to taste.

Nutrition:

Calories: 134

Total fat: 2.8 g

Carbohydrates: 22.5g

Protein: 4.4 g

Cholesterol: 0 mg

Sodium: 117 mg

Spinach and pasta shells

Servings: *8*

Ingredients

1-pound seashell pasta

1 (10 ounce) package frozen chopped spinach

2 tbsps. Olive oil

7 cloves garlic, minced

1 tsp. Dried red pepper flakes (optional)

Salt to taste

Directions

Cook the spinach and seashell pasta in a big pot of boiling, lightly salted water for 8-10 minutes. When the pasta becomes al dente, drain it and set aside.

In a big skillet over medium heat, sauté the red pepper flakes and garlic in hot oil for 5 minutes. When the garlic is slightly golden, mix in the spinach and pasta. Add salt and toss before serving.

Nutrition:

Calories: 248

Total fat: 4.9 g

Carbohydrates: 43.8g

Protein: 9 g

Cholesterol: 0 mg

Sodium: 30 mg

Summer penne pasta

Servings: *8*

Ingredients

2 medium tomato - peeled, seeded and chopped

Ground black pepper to taste

Salt to taste

Directions

Cut them into quarter-inch strips. Heat two tbsps. Of olive oil in a big skillet over medium heat. Sauté the bell peppers until they're soft but not browned.

Place the yellow squash and zucchini. Sauté for 2 minutes. Stir in the garlic and mushrooms. Sauté for 2 minutes more while stirring constantly. Add the tomatoes before removing the skillet from heat.

Place the pasta onto eight warmed plates. Pour the sauce over and sprinkle with pepper and salt.

Nutrition:

Calories: 264

Total fat: 5 g

Carbohydrates: 47.6g

Protein: 9.5 g

Cholesterol: 0 mg

Sodium: 10 mg <

Super-hot cereal mix

Servings: *10*

Preparation time 10 m

cooking time: *10 m*

 ingredients

5 c instant oatmeal

4 tbsps. Brown sugar

1 c raisins

3 tbsps. Dry milk powder

Directions

Mix together the dry fruit, oatmeal, dry milk, and brown sugar in a big bowl. Store them in an airtight jar or container until ready to use.

To serve the oatmeal, put 0.5-0.75 c of boiling water and a c of the cereal mix into a cereal bowl. Add more oatmeal mixture for a thicker oatmeal. Let it sit until it becomes thick.

Nutrition:

Calories: 215

Total fat: 2.6 g

Carbohydrates: 43g

Protein: 6.1 g

Cholesterol: < 1 mg <

Sodium: 118 mg

Sweet and salty granola

Servings: *16*

Preparation time 10 m

cooking time: 1 h

ingredients

3/4 c brown sugar

1/4 c water

3 c rolled oats

1/2 tsp. Salt

1 c chopped walnuts

2 tsps. Ground cinnamon

1 tbsp. Honey

2 tsps. Vanilla extract

Directions

Turn your oven to 2750 Fahrenheit (1350 Celsius) to preheat. Use a wax paper to cover a 10 x 15-inch pan.

In a microwave-safe bowl, combine water with brown sugar. To dissolve the sugar, cook it in microwave for around a minute. In a big bowl, mix the walnuts, oats, cinnamon, and salt together. Add the honey, vanilla extract, and sugar mixture. Blend well. Spread the mixture evenly to the pan. Squeeze small handfuls of the oat mixture together to make clusters.

Place the pan in the oven to bake the mixture for 20 minutes. Remove the pan from the oven. Use a spoon to stir the granola. Place the pan back to the oven. Bake for 25 minutes more until slightly browned. The granola will become hard as it cools.

Nutrition:

Calories: 139

Total fat: 5.9 g

Carbohydrates: 19.4g

Protein: 3.2 g

Cholesterol: 0 mg

Sodium: 76 mg

Zucchini pasta

Servings: 8

Ingredients

1-pound rotini pasta

5 small zucchinis, sliced

1/3 c olive oil

4 cloves garlic, minced

1 pinch crushed red pepper flakes

1/3 c chopped fresh parsley

Salt and pepper to taste

1/2 c grated parmesan cheese

Directions

In a big pot, cook the rotini pasta in boiling salted water until al dente or for 8-10 minutes. Drain the pasta and set aside.

In a medium-sized saucepan with lightly salted water, bring zucchini to a boil until it's tender or for 10 minutes.

Sauté hot pepper flakes and garlic in oil in a big skillet. Stir in the parsley and zucchini. Blend well. Simmer for 5-10 minutes before tossing with pasta. Add the salt, pepper, and parmesan cheese. Enjoy!

Nutrition:

Calories: 320

Total fat: 11.9 g

Carbohydrates: 44.7g

Protein: 10.5 g

Cholesterol: 4 mg

Sodium: 89 mg

Zucchini with farfalle

servings: 7

Ingredients

5 tbsps. Olive oil

5 small zucchinis, julienned

2 onions, minced

1 clove garlic, minced

2/3 c heavy whipping cream

1 (16 ounce) package farfalle pasta

2 tbsps. Grated parmesan cheese

Salt to taste

Freshly ground black pepper

2 tbsps. Grated parmesan cheese

Directions

In a big skillet over medium-high heat, quickly sauté the zucchini in oil until it turns golden. Remove the zucchini from the skillet. Set aside.

Sauté the garlic and onion until they turn golden. Add the whipping cream and stir. Turn up the heat to boil the cream sauce until it's reduced by 1/3.

Cook the farfalle pasta based on package instructions. Drain the pasta.

Mix the zucchini, pasta, half a c of parmesan, pepper, and salt into the sauce. Toss well until cooked through. Top with more cheese. Serve hot.

Nutrition:

Calories: 432

Total fat: 20.5 g

Carbohydrates: 53.2g

Protein: 11.5 g

Cholesterol: 34 mg

Sodium: 66 mg

Chapter 23: Vegetable &Vegan

Green Beans with Bacon

Preparation time: 30minutes

Cooking time: 6-8 hours

Serves 10

Ingredients:

12oz low-sodium bacon

29oz canned green beans

1 medium onion, chopped

½ cup maple syrup

¼ cup brown sugar

Directions

1. Fry bacon and onion in a skillet and transfer to a 5 quart or larger slow cooker.

2. Add remaining ingredients and stir well.

3. Cover and cook on LOW for 6 to 8 hours.

Nutrition: Calories 185, Fat 9g, Carbs 17g, Protein 12g, Fiber 1g, Potassium 125mg, Sodium 445mg

Coconut & Pecan Sweet Potatoes

Preparation time: 20 minutes

Cooking time: 4-5 hours

Serves 16

Ingredients:

4lb sweet potatoes, peeled and diced

½ cup pecans, chopped

½ cup unsweetened flaked coconut

½ cup butter, melted

1/3 cup sugar

1/3 cup brown sugar

½ tsp vanilla extract

¼ tsp low sodium salt

Directions

1. Place the sweet potatoes in a 5 quart or larger slow cooker.

2. Mix together the pecans, coconut, melted butter, both sugars, vanilla extract, and salt.

3. Toss the nut mixture with the sweet potatoes.

4. Cover and cook on LOW for 4 to 5 hours.

Nutrition: Calories 307, Fat 16g, Carbs 42g, Protein 3g, Fiber 5g, Potassium 419mg, Sodium 50mg

Veggie Bolognese

Preparation time: 20 minutes

Cooking time: 8-10 hours

Serves 32

Ingredients:

1 onion, diced

7 medium carrots, peeled & diced

2 green bell peppers, diced

3 small zucchinis, diced

2 cups mushrooms, roughly chopped

87oz canned crushed tomatoes

2 tbsp dried basil

1 tbsp dried oregano

1 tsp dried rosemary

1 whole bay leaf, crumbled

3 garlic cloves, minced

Directions

1. Place all ingredients into a 6-quart or larger slow cooker and mix well.

2. Cover and cook on LOW 8 to 10 hours.

Nutrition: Calories 43, Fat <1g, Carbs 10g, Protein 2g, Fiber 3g, Potassium 411mg, Sodium 112mg

Bombay Potatoes

Preparation time: 45 minutes

Cooking time: 4-6 hours

Serves 6

Ingredients:

3 tbsp olive oil

2 tsp mustard seeds

1 onion, peeled and diced

1 teaspoon Garam Masala Spice

1 tsp ground ginger

1 ½ tsp turmeric

½ tsp ground cumin

½ tsp chili powder

¼ tsp red chili flakes

3lb potatoes, peeled and diced into ½ inch cubes

14.5oz canned low-sodium diced tomatoes or fresh tomatoes

1 tsp low sodium salt

½ tsp freshly ground black pepper

¼ cup fresh cilantro, finely chopped

Directions

1. Cook the mustard seeds in a large skillet until they begin to pop.

2. Add the onions are spices and cook for a further 5 minutes.

3. Add the potatoes, tomatoes and onion mixture to a 6-quart slow cooker and cover.

4. Cook for 4 to 6 hours on LOW.

Nutrition: Calories 280, Fat 8g, Carbs 10g, Protein 2g, Fiber 3g, Potassium 911mg, Sodium 78mg

Potato & Broccoli Gratin

Preparation time: 20 minutes

Cooking time: 3-4 hours

Serves 6

Ingredients:

5 medium potatoes, sliced

2 cup broccoli florets, chopped

½ tsp freshly ground black pepper

½ tsp low sodium salt

¼ cup unsalted margarine

¼ cup all-purpose flour

1 medium onion, minced

1 garlic clove, minced

1 cup milk

1 cup low-sodium Cheddar cheese

Directions

1. Arrange the potato slices and broccoli florets in a 4 to 6-quart slow cooker.

2. Melt the margarine in a saucepan and add the flour to make a roux.

3. Gradually whisk in the milk, then add the garlic, onion, and cheese.

4. Pour the sauce over potatoes and cover.

5. Cover and cook on HIGH for 3 to 4 hours.

Nutrition: Calories 444, Fat 21g, Carbs 49g, Protein 2g, Fiber 7g, Potassium 1106mg, Sodium 378mg

Summer Squash with Bell Pepper and Pineapple

Preparation time: 15 minutes

Cooking time: 6-7 hours

Serves 6

Ingredients:

1lb summer squash, peeled and cubed

1lb zucchini squash, peeled and cubed

½ cup green bell pepper, chopped

1 8oz can unsweetened crushed pineapple

1 tsp ground cinnamon

1/3 cup brown sugar

1 tbsp butter, cut into small pieces

Directions

1. Mix all ingredients together and place in a 4 to 6-quart slow cooker.

2. Cover and cook on LOW for 6-7 hours or until squash is tender.

3. Serve immediately.

Nutrition: Calories 113, Fat 2g, Carbs 24g, Protein 2g, Fiber 2g, Potassium 381mg, Sodium 7mg

Slow Cooker Eggplant Lasagna

Preparation time: 20 minutes

Cooking time: 2-3 hours

Serves 8

Ingredients:

2 eggplants, peeled and sliced thin to resemble lasagna noodles

1 cup low-fat cottage cheese

1 ½ cup low-fat mozzarella cheese

1 egg

1 24oz jar sodium-free spaghetti sauce

1 tsp low-sodium salt

1 bell pepper, diced

1 onion, diced

Directions

1. Season the eggplants with salt and pepper, arrange on paper towels and allow excess moisture to drain away.

2. Mix the cottage cheese, mozzarella cheese, and egg in a bowl.

3. Pour ¼ of the tomato sauce in a 4 to 6-quart slow cooker.

4. Layer like lasagna with vegetables, cheese mix, and tomato sauce.

5. Cover and cook on LOW for 2 to 3 hours.

Nutrition: Calories 221, Fat 10g, Carbs 19g, Protein 14g, Fiber 3g, Potassium 349mg, Sodium 802mg

Chapter 24: Seafood

Salmon and Sweet Potato Chowder

Cooking Time: 4 hrs.

Servings: 4

INGREDIENTS

1 tbsp. Butter

1 minced clove of Garlic

1 chopped Onion

2 tsp. Dill Weed

3 tbsp. o all-purpose Flour

Ground Black Pepper

2 cups Milk

2 cups Sweet Potatoes (diced)

2 cups Chicken Broth

1 ½ cups Corn Kernels

1 tsp. Lemon Zest

12 ounces sliced Salmon Fillets

3 tbsp. Lemon Juice

DIRECTIONS

Sauté pepper, dill, garlic and onion in butter in a pan.

Add in the flour and cook for 2 mins.

Pour broth and then milk to the pan. Simmer.

Pour the mixture to the slow cooker and add the sweet potatoes.

Cook on "low" for 4 hrs.

Add in the salmon and cook again on "low" for 20 more mins.

Now, stir in the lemon zest, lemon juice along with the pepper.

Serve hot in heated bowls.

Nutrition: *391 Calories*

27 g Total Fat

94 mg Cholesterol

320 mg Sodium

39 mg Carbohydrates

7 g Dietary Fiber

37 g Protein

Sesame Salmon Fillets

Cooking Time: 30 minutes

Servings: 4

INGREDIENTS

2 tbsp. Sesame Oil

¼ tsp. Sea Salt

¼ tsp. Black Pepper (cracked)

1 tbsp. Vinegar

4 tsp. Sesame Seeds (black)

¼ tsp. Ginger (ground)

4 skinless Salmon fillets

DIRECTIONS

Coat the slow cooker with oil. Set the cooker on "high".

Place the salmon in the cooker. Drizzle the sesame seeds, pepper, salt and ginger on the salmon.

Turn after 3 mins and repeat the procedure.

Add vinegar and cook on "high" for 20 mins.

Transfer the salmon to a plate. Serve immediately

Nutrition: *319 Calories*

21 g Total Fats

81 mg Cholesterol

204 mg Sodium

31 g Carbohydrates

1 g Dietary Fiber

31 g Protein

Peppered Balsamic Cod

Servings: 4

Preparation time: 10 minutes

Cooking time: 2 hours

Ingredients:

1 1/2 pounds cod filets

2 teaspoons olive oil

1 teaspoon lemon zest

1/2 teaspoon cracked black peppercorns

2 tablespoons balsamic vinegar, reduced to a syrup

Cut a piece of foil large enough to wrap completely around the fish, or cut 4 smaller pieces to wrap the fish into individual packets. Brush the foil with 1 teaspoon of the oil. Arrange the fish in the center of the foil and brush with the remaining oil. Season evenly with the lemon zest and pepper. Drizzle with the balsamic vinegar. Fold the foil completely around the fish and crimp the edges to seal the package(s) completely.

Set the package in the slow cooker, cover with a lid, and cook on HIGH for 2 hours, or until the fish is completely cooked.

Serve at once.

Nutrition: Calories 201; Total Fat 5g; Saturated Fat 1g; Cholesterol 101mg; Sodium 121mg; Total Carbohydrates 1g; Dietary Fiber 1g; Protein 39g; Sugars 1g

Seafood Gumbo

Servings: 6

Preparation time: 25 minutes

Cooking time: 5 hours

Ingredients:

2 teaspoons olive oil

1/4 cup minced turkey ham (low sodium)

2 stalks celery, sliced

1 medium onion, sliced

1 green bell pepper, chopped

2 cloves garlic, minced

2 cups chicken broth (low sodium)

1 (14-ounce) can diced tomatoes, including juices

1 teaspoon Worcestershire sauce

1/4 teaspoon kosher salt

1 teaspoon dried thyme

1-pound shrimp (16/20), cleaned

1 pound fresh or frozen crabmeat, picked to remove cartilage

1 (10-ounce) package frozen okra, thawed

Directions:

Heat the oil in a sauté pan over medium-high heat. Add the ham and cook until crisp. With a slotted spoon, transfer the ham to a slow cooker.

Add the celery, onion, green pepper, and garlic to the sauté pan and cook over medium heat, stirring frequently, until the vegetables are tender, about 10 minutes. Transfer to the cooker and add the broth, tomatoes and their juices, Worcestershire, salt, and thyme.

Cover and cook on LOW for 4 hours. Add the shrimp, crabmeat, and okra, and cook on HIGH for 20 minutes or until the shrimp is bright pink and firm.

Serve at once in heated soup bowls.

Nutrition: Calories 155; Total Fat 5g; Saturated Fat 3g; Cholesterol 207mg; Sodium 313mg; Total Carbohydrates 16g; Dietary Fiber 5g; Protein 22g; Sugars 2g

Salmon Chowder with Sweet Potatoes and Corn

Servings: 4

Preparation time: 10 minutes

Cooking time: 4 hours

Ingredients:

1 tablespoon butter

1 onion, finely chopped

1 clove garlic, minced

2 teaspoons dill weed

Freshly ground black pepper

3 tablespoons all-purpose flour

2 cups chicken broth (low sodium)

2 cups milk

2 cups diced sweet potatoes

1 1/2 cups fresh or thawed frozen corn kernels

12 ounces salmon fillet, cut into chunks

1 teaspoon grated lemon zest

3 tablespoons lemon juice

Directions:

Melt the butter in a saucepan over medium heat. Add the onion, garlic, dill, and a pinch of pepper; sauté, stirring frequently, until the onion is tender. Add the flour and stir until thick and pasty, about 2 minutes. Whisk in the broth until there are no lumps, then stir in the milk, and bring to a simmer. Pour into the slow cooker and add the sweet potatoes and corn. Cover with a lid and cook on LOW for 4 hours, until the potatoes are very tender.

Stir in the salmon, replace the lid, and cook on LOW for 20 minutes, or until the salmon is cooked (145°F) and very hot. Stir in the lemon zest and season to taste with lemon juice and additional pepper.

Serve in heated soup bowls.

Nutrition: Calories 391; Total Fat 18g; Saturated Fat 9g; Cholesterol 94mg; Sodium 320mg; Total Carbohydrates 39g; Dietary Fiber 7g; Protein 37g; Sugars 17g

Mediterranean Fish Stew

Servings: 6

Preparation time: 15 minutes

Cooking time: 4 hours

Ingredients:

1 onion, sliced

1 leek, white and light green portion, sliced thin

4 cloves garlic, minced

1/2 cup dry white wine

1/4 cup water

4 bay leaves

1-piece orange peel, 2 inches, pith removed

1/2 teaspoon cracked black peppercorns

1 1/2 pounds haddock fillets

12 ounces shrimp (16/20), peeled and deveined

2 teaspoons extra-virgin olive oil for serving

2 tablespoons chopped parsley, flat leaf

Directions:

Make a bed of the onion, leek, and garlic in the slow cooker. Add the wine and water to the cooker. Scatter the bay leaves, orange peel, and peppercorns on top. Cover the cooker and cook on HIGH for 2 hours. Add the fish and the shrimp, replace the cover, and cook on HIGH for an additional 2 hours or until the fish is cooked through and the shrimps are bright pink and opaque. Remove and discard the bay leaves and orange peel.

Serve the fish and shrimp in heated soup bowls topped with the cooking liquid and vegetables. Drizzle with olive oil and garnish with parsley.

Nutrition: Calories 207; Total Fat 4g; Saturated Fat 0g; Cholesterol 168mg; Sodium 536mg; Total Carbohydrates 5g; Dietary Fiber 1g; Protein 32g; Sugars 0g

Tuna and Red Pepper Stew

Servings: 6

Preparation time: 15 minutes

Cooking time: 4 hours

1 tablespoon olive oil

1 onion, chopped

1 garlic clove, minced

1/4 teaspoon red pepper flakes, or more to taste

1/2 cup dry white wine

1 (14-ounce) can diced tomatoes

1-pound baby red potatoes, scrubbed

1 teaspoon paprika

2 pounds tuna fillet

2 roasted red bell peppers, seeded and cut into strips

3 tablespoons chopped cilantro for garnish

Directions:

Combine the oil, onions, garlic, red pepper flakes, wine, tomatoes, and potatoes, in a slow cooker. Cover and cook on HIGH for 2 hours. Add the tuna and the roasted peppers, season with the paprika, and replace the cover. Continue to cook on HIGH for another 2 hours or until the tuna is fully cooked.

Serve at once, topped with the cilantro.

Nutrition: Calories 107; Total Fat 3g; Saturated Fat 0g; Cholesterol 8mg; Sodium 200mg; Total Carbohydrates 15g; Dietary Fiber 2g; Protein 5g; Sugars 0g

Sweet and Sour Shrimp

Preparation time: 10 minutes

Cooking time: 5.5 hours

Serves 3-4

Ingredients:

1 cup Chinese pea pods, thawed

1 14oz can pineapple chunks

2 tablespoons cornstarch

3 tbsp sugar

1 cup chicken stock (see recipe)

½ cup reserved pineapple juice

1 tbsp low-sodium soy sauce

½ tsp ground ginger

1lb large cooked shrimp

2 tbsp cider vinegar

1 cup of rice, cooked

Directions

1. Place the pea pods and pineapple in a 4 to 6-quart slow cooker.

2. Blend the cornstarch and sugar with the chicken stock and pineapple juice and heat in a small saucepan until thickened.

3. Pour the sauce into the slow cooker and add the ginger and soy sauce.

4. Cover and cook on LOW for 3 to 4 hours.

5. Add the shrimp and vinegar and cook for a further 15 minutes.

6. Serve with the hot cooked rice.

Nutrition: Calories 395, Fat 2g, Carbs 61g, Protein 33g, Fiber 5g, Potassium 796mg, Sodium 215 mg

Salmon with Caramelized Onions

Preparation time: 20 minutes
Cooking time: 6 hours
Serves 6

Ingredients:

1lb salmon fillet, cut into small fillets

1 tbsp extra-virgin olive oil

½ large onion, thinly sliced

¼ tsp ground ginger

¼ tsp dried dill

¼ tsp low-sodium salt

¼ tsp black pepper

½ lemon, thinly sliced

Directions

1. Arrange the onions in the base of a 4 to 6-quart slow cooker.

2. Place each piece of salmon in an aluminum foil packet and sprinkle with spices and top with lemon slices.

3. Place the salmon packets on top of the onions in the slow cooker and cover.

4. Cook on LOW for 6 to 8 hours.

5. Serve the salmon on top of the onions.

Nutrition: Calories 215, Fat 11g, Carbs 7g, Protein 24g, Fiber 2g, Potassium 520mg, Sodium 200mg

Slow Cooker Shrimp in Tomato Sauce

Preparation time: 15 minutes

Cooking time: 4 hours

Serves 4

Ingredients:

1 14oz can of no-added sodium crushed tomatoes

1 6oz can of no-added salt tomato paste

1 garlic clove, minced

1 tsp low-sodium salt

2 tsp fresh basil, chopped

½ tsp dried oregano

¼ tsp freshly ground black pepper

½ tsp crushed red pepper flakes

2 tbsp fresh parsley, minced

1lb cooked shrimp, peeled and deveined

½ cup low-sodium Parmesan cheese, grated

4 cup cooked spaghetti

Directions

1. Place the tomatoes, tomato paste, garlic, salt, basil,

oregano, salt, black pepper, and crushed red pepper, into a 4 to 6-quart slow cooker. if using.

2. Cover and cook on LOW for 4 to 5 hours.

3. Add the shrimp and parsley and cook on HIGH for 10 minutes.

4. Serve the shrimp on top of the hot cooked pasta with low-sodium Parmesan cheese.

Nutrition: Calories 509, Fat 5g, Carbs 69g, Protein 48g, Fiber 7g, Potassium 629mg, Sodium 400mg

Fisherman's Stew

Preparation time: 20 minutes

Cooking time: 6-8 hours

Serves 8

Ingredients:

1 fillet of seabass, cod or other white fish, cubed

1 dozen each large shrimp, scallops, mussels & clams

1 28 ounces no-added salt crushed tomatoes with juice

1 8oz no-added salt tomato sauce

½ cup onion, chopped

1 cup dry white wine

1/3 cup olive oil

3 garlic cloves, minced

½ cup parsley, chopped

1 green pepper, chopped

1 hot pepper, chopped

½ tsp low sodium salt

1 tsp thyme

2 tsp basil

1 tsp oregano

½ tsp paprika

½ tsp cayenne pepper

Directions

1. Place all ingredients except seafood in a 4 to 6-quart slow cooker and cover.

2. Cook on LOW for 6 to 8 hours.

3. Add the fish about 30 minutes towards the end of the cooking time and turn up the heat to HIGH.

Nutrition: Calories 434, Fat 16g, Carbs 27g, Protein 39g, Fiber 4g, Potassium 714mg, Sodium 378mg

Fish Chowder

Preparation time: 15 minutes

Cooking time: 6 hours

Serves 6

Ingredients:

2lb white fish fillets, cut into 1-inch pieces

¼lb low-sodium bacon, diced

1 medium onion, chopped

4 medium red-skinned potatoes, peeled and cubed

2 cup water

1 low sodium salt

¼ tsp black pepper

1 12oz can evaporated milk

Directions

1. Fry the bacon in a skillet for a few minutes with the onion.

2. Add the bacon to the slow cooker with the remaining ingredients except for the evaporated milk.

3. Cover and cook on HIGH for 5 to 6 hours.

4. Add the milk during the last hour of cooking.

Nutrition: Calories 311, Fat 13g, Carbs 27g, Protein 14g, Fiber 12g, Potassium 911mg, Sodium 600mg

Shrimp Creole

Preparation time: 15 minutes

Cooking time: 4 hours

Serves 2-3

Ingredients:

1½ cup celery, diced

1¼ cup onion, chopped

1 cup bell pepper, chopped

1 8oz can no-added salt tomato sauce

1 28oz no-added salt can whole tomatoes

1 garlic clove, minced

½ tsp low-sodium salt

½ tsp salt-free Creole seasoning

¼ tsp freshly ground black pepper

6 drops Tabasco sauce

1lb shrimp, deveined and shelled

Directions
1. Place all the ingredients into a 3-quart slow cooker except the shrimp.

2. Cook 3 to 4 hours on high or 6 to 8 hours on low.

3. Add shrimp during last 30 minutes of cooking.

4. Serve over hot cooked rice

Nutrition: Calories 388, Fat 3g, Carbs 42g, Protein 52g, Fiber 8g, Potassium 874mg, Sodium 600mg

Chapter 25: Meat and poultry

Creamy Mushroom and Broccoli Chicken

Preparation time:15 minutes

Cooking time: 6 hours

Serves 6

Ingredients:

1 10.5oz can of low-sodium cream of mushroom soup

1 21oz can of low-sodium cream of Chicken Soup

2 whole cooked chicken breasts, chopped or shredded

2 cup milk

1lb broccoli florets

¼ tsp garlic powder

Directions
1. Place all ingredients to a 5 quart or larger slow cooker and mix well.

2. Cover and cook on LOW for 6 hours.

3. Serve with potatoes, pasta, or rice.

Nutrition: Calories 155, Fat 2g, Carbs 19g, Protein 12g, Fiber 2g, Potassium 755mg, Sodium 35mg

Chicken Curry

Preparation time: 10 minutes

Cooking time: 4 hours

Serves 4

Ingredients:

1lb skinless chicken breasts

1 medium onion, thinly sliced

1 15 oz can chickpeas, drained and rinsed well

2 medium sweet potatoes, peeled and diced

½ cup light coconut milk

½ cup chicken stock (see recipe)

1 15oz can sodium-free tomato sauce

2 tbsp curry powder

1 tsp low-sodium salt

½ cayenne powder

1 cup green peas

2 tbsp lemon juice

Directions

1. Place the chicken breasts, onion, chickpeas, and sweet potatoes into a 4 to 6-quart slow cooker.

2. Mix the coconut milk, chicken stock, tomato sauce, curry powder, salt, and cayenne together and pour into the slow cooker, stirring to coat well.

3. Cover and cook on Low for 8 hours or High for 4 hours.

4. Stir in the peas and lemon juice 5 minutes before serving.

Nutrition: Calories 302, Fat 5g, Carbs 43g, Protein 24g, Fiber 9g, Potassium 573mg, Sodium 800mg

Apple & Cinnamon Spiced Honey Pork Loin

Preparation time:20 minutes

Cooking time: 6 hours

Serves 6

Ingredients:

1 2-3lb boneless pork loin roast

½ tsp low-sodium salt

¼ tsp pepper

1 tbsp canola oil

3 medium apples, peeled and sliced

¼ cup honey

1 small red onion, halved and sliced

1 tbsp ground cinnamon

Directions

1. Season the pork with salt and pepper.

2. Heat the oil in a skillet and brown the pork on all sides.

3. Arrange half the apples in the base of a 4 to 6-quart slow cooker.

4. Top with the honey and remaining apples.

5. Sprinkle with cinnamon and cover.

6. Cover and cook on low for 6-8 hours until the meat is tender.

Nutrition: Calories 290, Fat 10g, Carbs 19g, Protein 29g, Fiber 2g, Potassium 789mg, Sodium 22mg

Lemon & Herb Turkey Breasts

Preparation time:25 minutes

Cooking time: 3 1/2 hours

Serves 12

Ingredients:

1 can (14-1/2 ounces) chicken broth

1/2 cup lemon juice

1/4 cup packed brown sugar

1/4 cup fresh sage

1/4 cup fresh thyme leaves

1/4 cup lime juice

1/4 cup cider vinegar

1/4 cup olive oil

1 envelope low-sodium onion soup mix

2 tbsp Dijon mustard

1 tbsp fresh marjoram, minced

1 tsp paprika

1 tsp garlic powder

1 tsp pepper

½ tsp low-sodium salt

2 2lb boneless skinless turkey breast halves

Directions

1. Make a marinade by blending all the ingredients in a blender.

2. Pour over the turkey and leave overnight.

3. Place the turkey and marinade in a 4 to 6-quart slow cooker and cover.

4. Cover and cook on HIGH for 3-1/2 to 4-1/2 hours or until a thermometer reads 165°.

Nutrition: Calories 219, Fat 5g, Carbs 3g, Protein 36g, Fiber 0g, Potassium 576mg, Sodium 484mg

Beef Chimichangas

Preparation time: 10minutes

Cooking time: 10-12 hours

Serves 16

INGREDIENTS:

Shredded beef

3lb boneless beef chuck roast, fat trimmed away

3 tbsp low-sodium taco seasoning mix

1 10oz canned low-sodium diced tomatoes

6oz canned diced green chilies with the juice

3 garlic cloves, minced

To serve

16 medium flour tortillas

Sodium-free refried beans

Mexican rice, sour cream, cheddar cheese

Guacamole, salsa, lettuce

Directions

1. Arrange the beef in a 5-quart or larger slow cooker.

2. Sprinkle over taco seasoning and coat well.

3. Add tomatoes and garlic and cover.

4. Cook on low for 10 to 12 hours.

5. When cooked remove the beef and shred.

6. Make burritos out of the shredded beef, refried beans, Mexican rice, and cheese.

7. Bake for 10 minutes at 350° f until brown.

8. Serve with salsa, lettuce, and guacamole.

Nutrition: calories 249, fat 18g, carbs 3g, protein 33g, fiber 5g, potassium 633mg, sodium 457mg

Short ribs

Preparation time: 5minutes

cooking time: 8 hours

serves 6

Ingredients:

3lb beef short ribs

½ cup red wine

1 tbsp olive oil

3 garlic cloves, minced

¼ cup brown sugar

Low-sodium salt and pepper to taste

Directions

1. Season ribs with salt and pepper.

2. Place ribs into a 5 quart or larger slow cooker.

3. Mix the red wine, olive oil, and garlic together and pour over ribs.

4. Cover and cook on low for 8 hours.

5. Remove the ribs and keep warm.

6. Transfer the juices to a small saucepan with the sugar and reduce by half to make a sauce to pour over the ribs.

Nutrition: calories 470, fat 26g, carbs 11g, protein 43g, fiber 0g, potassium 613mg, sodium 174mg

Meat loaf

Preparation time: 5 minutes

cooking time: 5-6 hours

serves 6

Ingredients:

2lb lean ground beef

2 whole eggs, beaten

¾ cup milk

¾ cup breadcrumbs

½ cup chicken broth (see recipe)

¼ cup onion, finely diced

3 garlic cloves, minced

1 tsp low-sodium salt

¼ tsp freshly ground black pepper

¼ cup low sodium chili sauce

Nonstick spray

Directions
1. Mix the beaten eggs, milk, oatmeal, spices, onion, garlic, and chicken broth until well combined.

2. Mix in the beef and place in a 5-quart or larger slow cooker, sprayed with nonstick spray.

3. Cover and cook on low for 5 to 6 hours.

4. Serve with low-sodium ketchup.

Nutrition: calories 280, fat 10g, carbs 9g, protein 37g, fiber 1g, potassium 648mg, sodium 325mg

Crockpot peachy pork chops

Preparation time: 30minutes

cooking time: 2-3 hours

serves 8

Ingredients:

4 large peaches, pitted and peeled

1 onion, finely minced

¼ cup ketchup

¼ cup low-sodium honey barbecue sauce

2 tbsp brown sugar

1 tbsp low sodium soy sauce

¼ tsp low-sodium garlic salt

½ tsp ground ginger

2lb boneless pork chops

3 tbsp olive oil

Directions

1. Puree the peaches with a blender.

2. Mix the peach puree with the onion, ketchup, barbecue sauce, brown sugar, soy sauce, salt, garlic salt, and ginger.

3. Brown the pork chops in a large skillet then transfer to a 6-quart or larger slow cooker.

4. Pour the sauce over the pork chops and cover.

5. Cook for 5 to 6 hours on high.

Nutrition: calories 252, fat 8g, carbs 18g, protein 26g, fiber 1g, potassium 710mg, sodium 325mg

Chicken avocado salad

Servings: 8

preparation time *8 m* | cooking time: *20 m*

ingredients

3 avocados - peeled, pitted and diced

1-pound grilled skinless, boneless chicken breast, diced

1/2 c finely chopped red onion

1/2 c chopped fresh cilantro

1/4 c balsamic vinaigrette salad dressing

Directions

Mix together the chicken, avocados, cilantro, and onion in a medium-sized bowl. Pour over the balsamic vinaigrette dressing. Toss lightly to coat all the ingredients.

Nutrition:

Calories: 252

Total fat: 17.5 g

Carbohydrates: 8.3g

Protein: 17.2 g

Cholesterol: 43 mg

Sodium: 130 mg

Chicken mango salsa salad with chipotle lime vinaigrette

Servings: *6*

Preparation time 30 m

cooking time: *30 m*

ingredients

1 mango - peeled, seeded and diced

2 roam (plum) tomatoes, chopped

1/2 onion, chopped

1 jalapeno pepper, seeded and chopped - or to taste

1/4 c cilantro leaves, chopped

1 lime, juiced

1/2 c olive oil

1/4 c lime juice

1/4 c white sugar

1/2 tsp. Ground chipotle chile powder

1/2 tsp. Ground cumin

1/4 tsp. Garlic powder

1 (10 ounce) bag baby spinach leaves

1 c broccoli coleslaw mix

1 c diced cooked chicken

3 tbsps. Diced red bell pepper

3 tbsps. Diced green bell pepper

2 tbsps. Diced yellow bell pepper

2 tbsps. Dried cranberries

2 tbsps. Chopped pecans

2 tbsps. Crumbled blue cheese

Directions

In a big bowl, combine the jalapeno pepper, juiced lime, mango, cilantro, tomatoes, and onion. Set the mixture aside.

In a separate bowl, whisk together the garlic powder, olive oil, cumin, a quarter c of lime juice, chipotle, and sugar. Set the mixture aside.

In another big bowl, toss together the cranberries, spinach, broccoli coleslaw mix, pecans, chicken, and yellow, green and red bell peppers.

Top with blue cheese and mango salsa. Make sure they're spread all over.

Drizzle the dressing over salad. Toss to serve.

Nutrition:

Calories: 317

Total fat: 22.3 g

Carbohydrates: 25g

Protein: 7.6 g

Cholesterol: 14 mg

Sodium: 110 mg

Chicken salad balsamic

Servings: 6

Preparation time 15 m

cooking time: *15 m*

ingredients

3 c diced cold, cooked chicken

1 c diced apple

1/2 c diced celery

2 green onions, chopped

1/2 c chopped walnuts

3 tbsps. Balsamic vinegar

5 tbsps. Olive oil

Salt and pepper to taste

Directions

Toss together the celery, chicken, onion, walnuts, and apple in a big bowl.

Whisk the oil together with the vinegar in a small bowl. Pour the dressing over the salad. Then add pepper and salt to taste.

Combine the ingredients thoroughly. Leave the mixture for 10-15 minutes. Toss once more and chill.

Nutrition:

Calories: 335

Total fat: 26.5 g

Carbohydrates: 6g

Protein: 19 g

Cholesterol: 55 mg

Sodium: 58 mg

Chicken salad with apples, grapes, and walnuts

Servings: 12

preparation time *25 m* | cooking time: *25 m*

ingredients

4 cooked chicken breasts, shredded

2 granny smith apples, cut into small chunks

2 c chopped walnuts, or to taste

1/2 red onion, chopped

3 stalks celery, chopped

3 tbsps. Lemon juice

1/2 c vanilla yogurt

5 tbsps. Creamy salad dressing (such as miracle whip®)

5 tbsps. Mayonnaise

25 seedless red grapes, halved

Directions

In a big bowl, toss together the shredded chicken, lemon juice, apple chunks, celery, red onion, and walnuts.

Get another bowl and whisk together the dressing, vanilla yogurt, and mayonnaise. Pour over the chicken mixture. Toss to coat. Fold the grapes carefully into the salad.

Nutrition:

Calories: 307

Total fat: 22.7 g

Carbohydrates: 10.8g

Protein: 17.3 g

Cholesterol: 41 mg

Sodium: 128 mg

Chicken strawberry spinach salad with ginger-lime dressing

Servings: 2

preparation time 10 m

cooking time: *30 m*

ingredients

2 tsps. Corn oil

1 skinless, boneless chicken breast half - cut into bite-size pieces

1/2 tsp. Garlic powder

1 1/2 tbsps. Mayonnaise

1/2 lime, juiced

1/2 tsp. Ground ginger

2 tsps. Milk

2 c fresh spinach, stems removed

4 fresh strawberries, sliced

1 1/2 tbsps. Slivered almonds

Freshly ground black pepper to taste

Directions

In a skillet, heat oil over medium heat. Add the chicken breast and garlic powder. Cook the chicken for 10 minutes per side. When the juices run clear, remove from heat and set aside.

Combine the lime juice, milk, mayonnaise, and ginger in a bowl.

Place the spinach on serving dishes. Top with strawberries and chicken. Then sprinkle with almonds. Drizzle the salad with the dressing. Add pepper and serve.

Nutrition:

Calories: 242

Total fat: 17.3 g

Carbohydrates: 7.5g

Protein: 15.8 g

Cholesterol: 40 mg

Sodium: 117 mg

Chickpea and quinoa salad with lemon and tahini

Servings: 4

preparation time 10 m

cooking time: *9 h 15 m*

ingredients

1/2 c dry garbanzo beans (chickpeas)

1/2 c uncooked quinoa, rinsed

1 c water

1/4 c chopped fresh parsley

1 shallot, chopped

1 clove garlic, minced

1/4 c lemon juice

2 tbsps. Tahini

1 tbsp. Olive oil

Sea salt and ground black pepper to taste

Directions

In a saucepan, put the garbanzo beans. Pour in water that's enough to cover the beans. Get another small saucepan and mix a c of water with the quinoa. Let both the beans and quinoa soak overnight.

The next day, drain the beans and fill the pan with fresh water. Over high heat, bring to a boil. Adjust to medium-low heat and cover the pan. Simmer for around 60 minutes until the beans become tender. Drain the beans and set aside. Let the quinoa a boil in its soaking water over high heat. Reduce to low heat. Simmer the quinoa for around 10 minutes until it's tender. Set the cooked quinoa aside.

In a mixing bowl, mix together the quinoa, garbanzo beans, and parsley. Set the mixture aside. Get another bowl and whisk together the tahini, shallot, olive oil, garlic, and lemon juice. Season with pepper and sea salt. Pour the dressing over the quinoa-bean mixture. Stir slowly and serve.

Nutrition:

Calories: 259

Total fat: 10.3 g

Carbohydrates: 34.3g

Protein: 9.6 g

Cholesterol: 0 mg

Sodium: 101 mg

Curry chicken salad

Servings: 6

Preparation time 10 m

cooking time: *10 m*

ingredients

3 cooked skinless, boneless chicken breast halves, chopped

3 stalks celery, chopped

1/2 c low-fat mayonnaise

2 tsps. Curry powder

Directions: Combine the chicken, curry powder, mayonnaise, and celery in a medium-sized bowl.

Nutrition:

Calories: 77

Total fat: 1.6 g

Carbohydrates: 1g <

Protein: 14 g

Cholesterol: 37 mg

Sodium: 46 mg

Grilled orange vinaigrette chicken salad

Servings: 6

Preparation time 15 m

cooking time: *35 m*

ingredients

1/2 c orange juice

1/2 c white wine vinegar

1/4 c olive oil

4 tbsps. Salt-free garlic and herb seasoning blend

1 1/2 tbsps. White sugar

1-pound skinless, boneless chicken breast halves

1 head romaine lettuce-rinsed, dried and chopped

1 (11 ounce) can mandarin oranges, drained

1 c chopped fresh broccoli

1 c chopped baby carrots

Directions

Set a grill on medium-high heat to preheat.

Whisk together the olive oil, orange juice, sugar, seasoning blend, and vinegar in a bowl. Reserve around half a c of the mixture for basting later.

Oil the grate of the grill lightly. Cook the chicken breast on the preheated grill until juices of the meat run clear or for 6-8 minutes per side. While grilling, baste constantly with half a c of the reserved sauce. Let the grilled chicken cool. Then cut the meat into strips. Discard the sauce.

Toss together the broccoli, lettuce, carrots, and oranges in a big bowl. Put the chicken strips on top of the salad. Drizzle with the remaining sauce. Serve.

Nutrition:

Calories: 239

Total fat: 11.1 g

Carbohydrates: 17.5g

Protein: 17.2 g

Cholesterol: 43 mg

Sodium: 69 mg

Savory pork

Cooking time: 9 hrs.

Servings: 2

Ingredients

½ tbsp. Extra-virgin olive oil

1 small sliced onion

8 small potatoes

½ tsp. Ground black pepper

Pinch of salt

½ tsp. Garlic powder

1 tbsp. Fresh sage (rubbed)

1 tbsp. Fresh rosemary (crushed)

1 tsp. Thyme (ground)

2 trimmed loin pork chops

15-ounces low-fat mushroom soup

¼ cup white wine

Directions

Place oil, potatoes and onion in the slow cooker. Sprinkle on seasoning.

Toss well to coat.

Remove fat from pork chops.

Place them over the vegetables in slow cooker.

In a bowl, mix wine and mushroom soup well.

Pour the mixture over the chops.

Cook on "low" heat for 6 hrs.

Serve hot.

Nutrition: *425 calories*

18.7 g total fat

66.7 mg cholesterol

819.4 mg sodium

33.2 mg carbohydrates

4.7 g dietary fiber

24.6 g protein

Smoked sausage and cabbage

Cooking time: 10 hrs.

Servings: 4-6

Ingredients

1 small head cabbage, shredded

1 large chopped onion

1 ½ pounds smoked turkey sausage

7 small red potatoes

1 cup apple juice

1 tbsp. Dijon mustard

1 tbs. Cider vinegar

2 tbsp. Brown sugar

1 tsp. Caraway seeds

Pepper to taste

Directions

In a 6 qt. Cooker, place onion, cabbage & sausage in a layer.

Cook on high for 10 mins

In a bowl, whisk rest of the ingredients.

Now, pour this mixture on the cabbage.

Sprinkle on the seasonings.

Cook on "low" for 10 hrs.

Serve hot.

Nutrition: *244.4 calories*

10.5 g total fat

75 mg cholesterol

945.5 mg sodium

18.3 mg carbohydrates

3.8 g dietary fiber

15.5 g protein

Roast beef

Cooking time: 5 hrs.

Servings: 5

Ingredients

2.5 lbs. chuck roast

1 tbsp. Worcestershire sauce

1 tbsp. Soy sauce

2 tbsp. Balsamic vinegar

1 chopped onion

Directions

In a slow cooker, pour all the ingredients over the roast.

Cook on "low" for 5 hrs.

Serve hot.

Nutrition: *293 calories*

8.2 g total fat

136.1 mg cholesterol

372 mg sodium

2.9 mg carbohydrates

0.3 g dietary fiber

48.6 g protein

Pork and pineapple roast

Cooking time: 7 hrs.

Servings: 4

Ingredients

2 pounds pork roast

1.5 tsp. Salt

½ tsp. Black pepper

20-ounces pineapple chunks

1 cup cranberries (chopped)

Directions

Season the roast on all sides.

Place all the ingredients in the slow cooker.

Cook on "low" for 7 hrs.

Serve hot.

Nutrition: *465.1 calories*

10.7 g total fat

134.3 mg cholesterol

107.2 mg sodium

44.3 mg carbohydrates

3 g dietary fiber

47.49 g protein

Slow cooked artichoke chicken

Servings: 6

Preparation time: 20 minutes

Cooking time: 5 to 6 hours

Ingredients:

2 pounds boneless skinless chicken pieces

1 teaspoon paprika

1 teaspoon cayenne pepper

2 tablespoons olive oil

3 tablespoons white balsamic vinegar

2 cloves garlic minced

2 leeks, white and light green portions only, sliced into 1/2-inch pieces

8 ounces frozen artichoke hearts, thawed

1 cup white wine or chicken broth (low sodium)

Directions:

Season chicken pieces with paprika and cayenne.

Heat the oil in a sauté pan over medium-high heat. Add the chicken pieces, working in batches, and brown on all sides, about 2 minutes on each side. Transfer to the slow cooker.

Add the balsamic vinegar, garlic, and leeks to sauté pan and stir together for 1 minute; stir in artichoke hearts and white wine or broth. Pour the contents of the pan over the chicken in slow cooker. Cover and cook on low for 5 to 6 hours or until the chicken is cooked through and tender.

Serve at the chicken on heated plates with the artichokes, leeks, and some of the broth.

Nutrition: calories 160; total fat 7g; saturated fat 1g; cholesterol 35mg; sodium 457mg; total carbohydrates 10g; dietary fiber 3g; protein 15g; sugars 0g

Curried pork with apple and squash

Servings: 4

Preparation time: 15 minutes

Cooking time: 6 hours

Ingredients:

2 teaspoons olive oil

4 boneless loin pork chops, trimmed

Freshly ground black pepper to taste

1 onion, sliced thin

1 garlic clove, minced

1 red bell pepper, cut into thin strips

2 teaspoons curry powder

1/2 teaspoon ground cumin

1/2 teaspoon ground cinnamon

1/2 cup coconut milk (light)

1/2 cup chicken broth (low sodium)

1 tart apple, cored and diced (granny smith, for example)

1 cup thawed frozen or fresh cubed squash

2 tablespoons chopped parsley or cilantro for garnish

Directions:

Heat the oil in a skillet over medium high heat. Add the pork chops and cook until golden brown on both sides, about 6 minutes total. Transfer the pork chops to a slow cooker and season with pepper.

Return the pan to medium heat. Add onion, garlic, bell pepper, curry powder, cumin, and cinnamon; sauté, stirring frequently, until the peppers are tender, about 4 minutes. Pour this mixture over the pork. Add the coconut milk, broth, apple, and squash. Cover the cooker with a lid. Cook on low heat for 6 hours, or until the pork is thoroughly cooked and very tender.

Serve the pork on heated plates topped with the vegetables and sauce and garnish with parsley or cilantro.

Nutrition: calories 322; total fat 17g; saturated fat 8g; cholesterol 74mg; sodium 350mg; total carbohydrates 10g; dietary fiber 3g; protein 19g; sugars 1g

Lemon-scented pork roast with olives and turnips

Servings: 8

Preparation time: 30 minutes

Cooking time: 8

Ingredients:

1-pound purple-top turnips, cut into 2-inch pieces

8 medium carrots, cut into 2-inch pieces

1 large onion, sliced

1 (14-ounce) can diced tomatoes, drained

1 lemon, zest and juice

4 cloves garlic, sliced

3 bay leaves

3 1/2 pounds pork loin roast, trimmed

1/4 teaspoon kosher salt

1/2 teaspoon freshly ground pepper

2 tablespoons kalamata olives, pitted and chopped

directions:

Combine the turnips, carrots, onion, tomatoes, lemon zest and juice, garlic, and bay leaves in a slow cooker. Put the pork on top and season with salt and pepper. Cover and cook on LOW for 8 hours or until the pork is very tender.

Transfer the pork to a cutting board and let it rest for 10 minutes before slicing. Remove and discard the bay leaves.

Transfer the vegetables to a serving plate or platter with a slotted spoon. Skim any fat from the cooking liquid, and then stir in olives. Slice the pork and serve with the vegetables and the sauce.

Nutrition: calories 317; total fat 9g; saturated fat 6g; cholesterol 106mg; sodium 174mg; total carbohydrates 12; dietary fiber 5g; protein 49; sugars 2g

Beef with Carrots and Turnips

Cooking time: 8 hrs.

Servings: 12

Ingredients

1 tbsp. Kosher salt

2 tsp. Cinnamon (ground)

½ tsp. Allspice (ground)

½ tsp. Pepper (ground)

¼ tsp. Cloves (ground)

3 ½ pounds chuck roast

2 tbsp. Olive oil (extra virgin)

1 chopped onion

3 sliced cloves garlic

1 cup red wine

28 ounces whole tomato

5 sliced carrots

2 diced turnips

Chopped basil

Directions

Mix all dry spices in a bowl. Season the beef with the spice mixture.

In a skillet, brown the beef for 5 mins in oil.

Remove it and place it into the slow cooker.

In same pan, sauté onion and garlic.

Add the wine and tomatoes.

Boil the wine mixture.

Transfer the wine mixture to the slow cooker.

Cook them on "low" for 8 hrs.

Serve it hot after slicing the beef.

Nutrition: 318 calories 11 g total fat 99 mg cholesterol 538 mg sodium 13 mg carbohydrates 3 g dietary fiber 35 g protein

Pepper steak

Cooking time: 9 hrs.

Servings: 6

Ingredients

1 ½ pounds boneless beef steaks

2 diced onions

1 chopped clove garlic

½ tsp. Chopped ginger

½ cup beef broth

3 tbsp. Tamari sauce

¼ cup cold water

2 green and 2 red (sliced) bell peppers

2 sliced tomatoes

Directions

Cut the beef into 6 equal pieces.

In a bowl, combine ginger, tamari sauce and garlic. Marinate the beef for 2 hrs. At least.

In the slow cooker, spread pepper and onion on the bottom.

Place beef along with the marinade in the slow cooker.

Pour broth into the slow cooker.

Cook on "low" for 8 hrs.

Serve the beef on heated plates

Nutrition: 349 calories 23 g total fat 107 mg cholesterol 371 mg sodium 11 mg carbohydrates 2 g dietary fiber 36 g protein

Beef brisket

Cooking time: 8 hrs.

Servings: 12

Ingredients

5 pounds beef brisket (trimmed)

2 minced cloves garlic

½ tsp. Black pepper

2 tbsp. Brown sugar

2 tsp. Paprika (smoked)

2 sliced onions

1 ½ cup beef broth

3 diced carrots

3 sliced parsnips

14 ounces diced tomatoes

Directions

In a bowl, mix paprika, brown sugar, black pepper and garlic.

Coat beef with paprika mixture and place it into the slow cooker.

Now, place all the remaining ingredients in layers.

Cook on "low" for 8 hrs.

Transfer the beef to a cutting board.

Leave it for 10 mins at least.

Slice and serve with the cooked vegetables.

Nutrition: 283 calories 15 g total fat 128 mg cholesterol 385 mg sodium 7 mg carbohydrates 2 g dietary fiber 44 g protein

Pork with squash and apples

Cooking time: 6 hrs. 15 minutes

Servings: 4

Ingredients

4 boneless pork chops

Ground black pepper

1 sliced onion

2 tsp. Olive oil

1 minced clove garlic

1 sliced red bell pepper

½ tsp. Ground cumin

½ tsp. Ground cinnamon

½ cup chicken broth

½ cup coconut milk

1 diced tart apple

1 cup cubed squash

2 tbsp. Chopped parsley

Directions

Sauté the pork chops in oil for 6 mins.

Transfer them to slow cooker.

In same pan, sauté rest of the ingredients except apple, broth, squash and coconut milk.

Pour the mixture into the slow cooker.

Now, add the rest of the ingredients.

Cook on "low" for 6 hrs.

Serve the pork chops on heated plates after garnishing with parsley.

Nutrition: 322 calories 25 g total fat 74 mg cholesterol 350 mg sodium 10 mg carbohydrates 3 g dietary fiber 19 g protein

Lemony pork roast

Cooking time: 8 hrs. 15 minutes

Servings: 8

Ingredients

4 boneless pork chops

Ground black pepper

1 sliced onion

2 tsp. Olive oil

1 minced clove garlic

1 sliced red bell pepper

½ tsp. Ground cumin

½ tsp. Ground cinnamon

½ cup chicken broth

½ cup coconut milk

1 diced tart apple

1 cup cubed squash

2 tbsp. Chopped parsley

Directions

Place all ingredients except pork chops in the slow cooker.

Put the pork chops in afterwards.

Cook on "low" for 8 hrs.

When cooked, transfer the pork to a cutting board.

Leave it for 10 mins and then slice.

Transfer the pork and vegetables to heated plates and serve.

Nutrition: 317 calories 15 g total fat 106 mg cholesterol 174 mg sodium 12 mg carbohydrates 5 g dietary fiber 49 g protein

Chile Verde

Servings: 6

Preparation time: 15 minutes

Cooking time: 8 hours

Ingredients:

3 /2 pounds pork shoulder roast, trimmed and cut into bite-sized pieces

1 cup beef broth (low sodium)

2 cups cubed yellow potatoes

2 poblano chiles, seeded and cut into strips

3 green chiles, seeded and cut into strips

1 cup chopped tomatillos

4 cloves garlic, minced

1 medium onion, diced

1/4 teaspoon black pepper

1/2 teaspoon ground cumin

6 corn tortillas, steamed or griddled

Directions:

Combine the pork, broth, potatoes, poblanos, green chiles, tomatillos, garlic, onion, pepper, and cumin in a slow cooker and stir to distribute the ingredients evenly.

Cover with a lid and cook on low for 8 hours, or until the pork is very tender.

Steam or griddle the tortillas just before serving. To steam, wrap the tortillas in foil and place in the oven. To griddle, heat a dry skillet over medium heat. Add the tortillas one at a time, cooking for about 30 seconds on each side. Serve in a napkin-lined basket to keep them warm.

Serve the chile in heated bowls, topped with fresh cilantro and accompanied with the tortillas.

Nutrition: calories 452; total fat 19g; saturated fat 8g; cholesterol 202mg; sodium 269mg; total carbohydrates 25g; dietary fiber 5g; protein 50g; sugars 3g

Caribbean Pork Stew

Servings: 4

Preparation time: 15 minutes

Cooking time: 7 hours 15 minutes

Ingredients:

1 1/2 pounds pork loin, cubed

1 tablespoon dried thyme leaves

1/4 teaspoon ground allspice

Freshly ground white pepper

1-pound Yukon gold potatoes, peeled and quartered

3 carrots, cut into 2-inch pieces

1-piece (2-inch) ginger root, peeled and finely chopped

1 clove garlic, finely chopped

2 teaspoons Worcestershire sauce

1 cup diced tomatoes

1/2 cup scallions, sliced thin, for serving

Directions:

Combine the pork with the thyme, allspice, and pepper. Toss to coat evenly.

Put the potatoes, carrots, ginger, and garlic in the slow cooker. Add the pork and season with the Worcestershire sauce. Pour the tomatoes on top. Cover with a lid and cook on LOW for 7 hours or on HIGH for 4 hours.

Just before serving, add the scallions to the stew. Serve in heated bowls at once.

Nutrition: Calories 394; Total Fat 12g; Saturated Fat 8g; Cholesterol 123mg; Sodium 150mg; Total Carbohydrates 24g; Dietary Fiber 6g; Protein 57g; Sugars 4g

Smoked Paprika Goulash

Servings: 8

Preparation time: 40 minutes

Cooking time: 5 hours

Ingredients:

4 tablespoons smoked Hungarian paprika

2 teaspoons dried thyme

1 teaspoon coarsely ground black pepper

1 1/4 pounds pork loin, trimmed and cubed

1 tablespoon olive oil

3 onions, sliced

3 cloves garlic, chopped

3/4 cup water

3/4 cup tomato purée

1 cup Greek-style yogurt

Directions:

Mix together paprika, thyme, and pepper in a large bowl. Toss the pork cubes in the paprika mixture until evenly coated.

Heat 1 tablespoon oil in a sauté pan over medium-high heat. Add the onions and garlic and cook, stirring frequently, until tender and translucent, about 4 minutes. Add the pork and continue to cook, stirring occasionally, until the pork is stiffened and changes color, about 6 minutes. Transfer to the slow cooker.

Add the water and tomato puree to the sauté pan and stir well to release any browned bits. Pour over the pork.

Cover with a lid and cook on LOW for 8 hours, or until the pork is tender enough to fall apart.

Serve at once, accompanied with a dollop of yogurt, if using.

Nutrition: Calories 149; Total Fat 6g; Saturated Fat 3g; Cholesterol 40mg; Sodium 122mg; Total Carbohydrates 6g; Dietary Fiber 2g; Protein 21g; Sugars 4g

Chicken in Italian Sauce

Cooking time: 4 hrs. 20 minutes

Servings: 2

Ingredients

6 oz. Chicken breast (skinless and boneless)

Olive oil

¼ tsp. Kosher salt

¼ sliced green bell pepper

1/8 tsp. Ground black pepper

1 minced clove garlic

½ chopped yellow onion

½ tsp. Italian seasoning

7.5 oz. Diced tomatoes (unsalted)

1/8 cup red wine

Directions

Coat the chicken with pepper and salt.

Sauté chicken in oil for 6 mins. Transfer the chicken to a plate.

In slow cooker, pour ½ tbsp. Olive oil and heat on "high."

Sauté bell pepper, garlic and onion for 5 mins.

Add the tomatoes.

Cook on "low" for 2 hrs.

Cook continuously for next 20 mins but uncovered.

Add the chicken into the slow cooker.

Cook again on "low" for 2 hrs.

Serve immediately.

Nutrition: *281 calories*

8 g total fats

109 mg cholesterol

733 mg sodium

10 g carbohydrates

3 g dietary fiber

38 g protein

Pork chops and white beans

Cooking time: 4 hrs.

Servings: 2

Ingredients

1 ½ tsp. Olive oil

¼ tsp. Black pepper

½ diced carrot

¼ cup chicken broth (low sodium)

¼ tsp. Rosemary (dried)

¼ tsp. Kosher salt

2 pork chops (boneless)

½ diced yellow onion

1 minced clove garlic

7.5 oz. Cannellini beans

Chopped parsley

Directions

Season the chops with pepper and salt.

Sauté them in oil for 3 min on each side.

Transfer them to a plate.

In same pan, sauté rest of the ingredients except parsley.

Cook for 4 mins.

Transfer the cooked mixture to the slow cooker along with the broth.

Cook on "low" for 2 hrs.

Add the tomatoes along with the herbs and beans.

Cook for 1 more hour on low.

Place the pork into the slow cooker.

Cook for 10 mins on "high".

Serve after garnishing with parsley.

Nutrition: 458 calories 21 g total fats 78 mg cholesterol 357 mg sodium 34 mg carbohydrates 8 g dietary fiber 33 g protein

Chapter 26: Desserts

Homemade Granola

Cooking time: 55 minutes

Servings: 5

Ingredients

1/8 cup brown sugar

1 tbsp. Water

½ tsp. Vanilla extract

½ tbsp. Vegetable oil

½ cup raisins

½ tsp. Cinnamon (ground)

2 cups oats (rolled)

¼ cup milk (low fat)

¼ cup dates (chopped)

Directions

Except for raisins and dates, mix all the ingredients in a bowl. Make sure sugar is thoroughly dissolved.

Grease the slow cooker and set it on "high". Cook the granola for 30 mins uncovered.

Turn the slow cooker off.

Add the raisins and dates and allow the granola to cool. Serve with milk

Nutrition: *205 calories*

5 mg cholesterol

440 mg sodium

41 mg carbohydrates

3 g dietary fiber

7 g protein

Apple with oatmeal

Cooking time: 10 hrs. 15 minutes

Servings: 8

Ingredients

2 cups dry oats (steel cut)

2 cups chopped apples

1 cup of dried cranberries (sweetened)

3 cup water

1 cup milk (low fat)

1 tbsp. Ground cinnamon

1 tsp. Pie spice (pumpkin)

2 tsp. Margarine

½ cup o sliced almonds

½ cup pecans

Directions

Place margarine in the cooker.

Except nuts, place all the ingredients into the cooker.

On "warm" setting, cook for 10 hrs. Serve with nuts

Nutrition: *264.5 calories*

7.1 g total fat

1.5 cholesterol

28.7 mg sodium

47.8 mg carbohydrates

6.9 g dietary fiber

8.4 g protein

Apple crisp

Cooking time: 4 hrs. 10 minutes

Servings: 5

Ingredients

1 cup oatmeal

1 cup brown sugar

2 tbsp. Flour (all purpose)

1 tbsp. Sugar (granulated)

1 stick butter

1 tsp. Cinnamon

1 lb. Apples (granny smith)

Directions

Peel and thinly slice the apples.

Add flour and granulated sugar to the apples.

Coat them well.

Place them in the slow cooker.

Now, add remaining ingredients except oats.

Last, sprinkle the oatmeal on the apples.

Cook on "high" for 4 hrs.

Serve hot.

Nutrition: *278 calories*

10 g total fat

134 mg cholesterol

270 mg sodium

8 mg carbohydrates

0 g dietary fiber

32 g protein

Pecan and banana cake

Cooking time: 6 hrs. 10 minutes

Servings: 3

Ingredients

½ cup pastry flour (wheat)

½ tbsp. Sugar

¼ cup unbleached flour (all purpose)

1 tsp. Kosher salt

¾ tsp. Baking powder

1 egg white and 1 egg

¾ cup milk ()

½ sliced banana

1 tbsp. Canola oil

¼ cup chopped pecans

Directions

In a bowl, mix both flours, sugar, salt and baking powder.

In another bowl, beat the egg white and egg with milk and 1 tbsp. Of oil. Mash the banana and add to the eggs. Add pecans.

Slowly, mix the egg mixture into the dry ingredients.

Set parchment paper in the slow cooker.

Now, pour the prepared banana batter in the slow cooker.

Cook on "low" for 5 hrs.

Turn the slow cooker off.

Keep aside to let the cake stand for 10 mins.

Serve.

Nutrition: *278 calories*

13 g total fats

34 mg cholesterol

262 mg sodium

34 mg carbohydrates

4 g dietary fiber

9 g protein

Banana and almond spread

Cooking time: 1 hrs. 10 minutes

Servings: 2

Ingredients

2 bananas (large)

2 cups almond milk (unsweetened)

2 tbsp. Wheat germ

2 tbsp. Almond butter (unsalted)

¼ tsp. Cinnamon (ground)

¼ tsp. Vanilla extract

6 ice cubes

Directions

Puree all the ingredients in a blender.

Pour this puree in the slow cooker.

Cook on "low" for 1 hr.

Serve on muffins or bread.

Nutrition: *338 calories*

13 g total fats

0 mg cholesterol

153 mg sodium

52 mg carbohydrates

8 g dietary fiber

10 g protein

Coconut pudding

Cooking time: 6 hrs. 10 minutes

Servings: 4

Ingredients

1/8 tsp. Salt

½ cup rice (white)

½ quart soy milk

½ cup sugar

1/16 cup coconut (shredded)

¼ cup margarine (vegan)

½ tsp. Cinnamon

Directions

Place all ingredients in the slow cooker.

Cook on "low" for 6 hrs. Serve.

Nutrition: *357 calories*

14 g total fats

137 mg sodium

0 mg cholesterol

52 g carbohydrates

1.5 g dietary fiber

6 g protein

Almond and chocolate bars

Cooking time: 2 hrs.

Servings: 8

Ingredients

14 oz. Chocolate chips (semisweet)

2 cups almonds (chopped)

Directions

Place all the ingredients in the slow cooker.

Cook on "low" for 1 hr. Stir thoroughly every 15 mins.

Arrange a sheet of wax paper.

Spread the chocolate on the wax paper.

Let the chocolate cool and slice it in the shape of bars.

Serve.

Nutrition: *303 calories*

20.5 g total fats

5.5 mg sodium

0 mg cholesterol

34 g carbohydrates

4.5 g dietary fiber

4.5 g protein

Berry yogurt

Cooking time: 1 hr. Servings: 3

Ingredients

¾ cup blueberries

¾ cup strawberries (chopped)

¾ cup raspberries

¾ tsp. Lemon zest (grated)

¾ tsp. Orange zest (grated)

¾ tbsp. Balsamic vinegar

Juice ¼ orange

1 ½ cup Greek yogurt (low fat)

¼ tsp. Vanilla extract

3 tbsp. Sliced almonds (toasted)

Black pepper (cracked)

Directions

Place all the ingredients except yogurt and almonds in the slow cooker.

Cook on "low" for 1 hr.

Mash the berries.

Divide the yogurt in bowls.

Garnish with berry sauce and almonds.

Serve.

Nutrition: *163 calories*

4 g total fats

47 mg sodium

5 mg cholesterol

20 g carbohydrates

5 g dietary fiber

14 g protein

Hot fondue

Cooking time: 1 hr. *servings: 8*

Ingredients

¼ corn syrup (light)

½ cup soy milk

½ cup margarine (vegan)

½ tbsp. Vanilla extract

8 oz. Chocolate chips (semisweet and dark)

Salt

Directions

Place all the ingredients except vanilla and chocolate chips in the slow cooker.

Cook on "low" for 1 hr.

Stir once and again cook for another hr. on "low". Add in rest of the ingredients. Mix well so that chocolate will melt thoroughly.

Serve with fruit.

Nutrition: *318 calories*

25 g total fats

16 mg sodium

0 mg cholesterol

26 g carbohydrates

1.5 g dietary fiber

1.5 g protein

Crunchy pears

Cooking time: 2 hrs. 10 minutes

Servings: 3

Ingredients

2 ½ cups chopped pear

½ tbsp. Lemon juice

1 tbsp. Maple syrup

¼ tsp. Nutmeg (grated)

1 tsp. Cornstarch

½ cup granola (homemade)

Canola oil

Directions

Coat the slow cooker with canola oil.

Place all the ingredients in the cooker.

Cook on "low" for 2 hrs.

Sprinkle on the granola and leave it for 10 mins.

Serve hot.

Nutrition: *201 calories*

0 g total fats

7 mg sodium

0 mg cholesterol

38 g carbohydrates

6 g dietary fiber

4 g protein

Peanut cake

Cooking time: 2 hrs

Servings: 4

Ingredients

½ cup flour (almond)

½ cup brown sugar

¼ tsp. Baking soda

1/3 cup water

½ tsp. Baking powder

½ cup peanut butter (low sodium)

½ tsp. Vanilla extract

Directions

Mix all the dry ingredients in a bowl.

In another bowl, combine all the wet ingredients.

Combine all ingredients gradually.

Coat the slow cooker with oil.

Pour the mixture in.

Cook on "low" for 1 hr.

Serve.

Nutrition: *281 calories*

11 g total fats

214 mg sodium

0 mg cholesterol

30 g carbohydrates

1.5 g dietary fiber

5.5 g protein

CHAPTER 27: 21 DAY MEAL PLAN

DAY	BREAKFAST	LUNCH/DINNER	DESSERT
22.	Apple Cinnamon Oatmeal	Spaghetti with Garlic and Basil	Homemade Granola
23.	Autumn Apple Salad	Spicy Pasta	Apple with Oatmeal
24.	Banana, Chocolate, and Almond	Spinach and Pasta Shells	Apple Crisp
25.	Banana Nut Oatmeal	Summer Penne Pasta	Pecan and Banana Cake
26.	Beer Batter Crepes	Super-Hot Cereal Mix	Banana and Almond Spread
27.	Best Bircher Muesli	Sweet and Salty Granola	Coconut Pudding

28.	Swiss Oatmeal	Zucchini Pasta	Almond and Chocolate Bars
29.	Blueberry Lemon Breakfast Quinoa	Green Beans with Bacon	Berry Yogurt
30.	Blueberry Oatmeal	Coconut & Pecan Sweet Potatoes	Hot Fondue
31.	Bramboracky (Czech Savory Potato Pancakes	Veggie Bolognese	Crunchy Pears
32.	Broiled Grapefruit	Bombay Potatoes	Peanut Cake
33.	Brown Rice Breakfast Porridge	Potato & Broccoli Gratin	Homemade Granola
34.	Caprese on a Stick	Summer Squash with Bell Pepper and Pineapple	Apple with Oatmeal

35.	Carrot Cake Oatmeal	Slow Cooker Eggplant Lasagna	Apple Crisp
36.	Cinnamon Stove Top Granola	Salmon and Sweet Potato Chowder	Pecan and Banana Cake
37.	Classic Hash Browns	Sesame Salmon Fillets	Banana and Almond Spread
38.	Coconut Granola	Peppered Balsamic Cod	Coconut Pudding
39.	Cranberry-Orange Spiced Oatmeal	Seafood Gumbo	Almond and Chocolate Bars
40.	Creamy Apple Cinnamon Raisin Oatmeal	Salmon Chowder with Sweet Potatoes and Corn	Berry Yogurt

41.	Crunchy Pumpkin Pie Granola	Mediterranean Fish Stew	Hot Fondue
42.	Dad's Kentucky Home Fries	Creamy Mushroom and Broccoli Chicken	Crunchy Pears

CONCLUSION

Here we come to the end of the book. I hope that this attempt of encouraging you to live a healthy lifestyle by incorporating the low sodium Diet will help you improve your health and achieve your weight loss goals as well as motivate you to stay on the Diet.

Low sodium meals cooked in slow cookers won't just save your precious time but will also reduce the hassle of being physically present in the kitchen. You come home from work or play to delicious and healthy meals. However, as suggested earlier, it is recommended to do the preparation for cooking in advance, preferably the previous night. Next morning all you have to do is dump the meals in a slow cooker, adjust the heat settings and that is it!

Each recipe listed in the book will help you achieve your health and fitness goals and provide most of the nutrients that the body needs to function. Your body won't be deprived of any micronutrient or macronutrient. The Low sodium will also assist in striking the right balance between saturated and unsaturated fats.

Made in United States
Troutdale, OR
12/04/2024